TABLE OF CONTENTS

ABOUT THIS BOOK 6

CHAPTER ONE – OPTION TRADING AND INVESTMENT 11

UNDERSTANDING OPTIONS IN 2021   12

KNOWING OPTION ESSENTIALS   13

GETTING COMFORT WITH OPTION MECHANICS 15

RECOGNIZING RISKS AND REWARDS OF OPTIONS   16

INTEGRATE OPTIONS INTO YOUR ROUTINE   17

ADDING OPTIONS TO YOUR ANALYSIS   18

TRYING OUT INVESTING AND TRADING STRATEGIES   19

PUTTING OPTIONS TO WORK   20

UNDERSTANDING THE OPTION STYLES   21

USING OPTIONS TO LIMIT YOUR RISKS   22

APPLICATION OF OPTIONS TO SECTORAL APPROACHES 23

EXISTENCE OF OPTIONS USING ETFS AS SECURITY   23

USING OPTIONS IN DIFFICULT MARKETS 23

REDUCING YOUR DIRECTIONAL BIAS   24

BENEFITTING WHEN MARKETS ARE EVERYWHERE   25

CONSIDERING YOUR OBSTACLES 25

CHAPTER TWO – STRATEGIES FOR OPTION TRADING 2021 26

MONITORING OPTION GREEK CHANGES 26

TRACKING PREMIUM MEASURES 27

CHANGING VOLATILITY AND OPTION PRICES   28

PAPER TRADING AN APPROACH   30

USE OF TRADING SYSTEMS 32

PERFORMING A BACKTEST 33

ADDING RISK MANAGEMENT TO A BACKTEST   38

SHIFTING FROM KNOWLEDGE TO MASTERY   41

SETTING THE RIGHT PACE 42

REALIZE MASTERY THROUGH LONGEVITY   45

CHAPTER THREE – TOP TEN OPTION STRATEGIES...**49**

MARRIED PUT   50

COLLAR   50

LONG PUT TRADER 50

LEAPS CALL INVESTOR   51

DIAGONAL SPREAD 51

CALL RATIO BACKSPREAD 52

LONG PUT BUTTERFLY   52

TEN DOS AND DON'TS IN OPTION TRADING   53

CHAPTER FOUR – HOW TO EARN 15000 PER MONTH **65**

CAN YOU MAKE LIVING SELLING OPTIONS?   65

SO HOW MUCH CAN YOU EARN?   66

HOW MUCH MONEY DO I NEED TO BEGIN TRADING OPTIONS FOR A LIVING?   67

BUT WHAT IF YOU CAN TAKE RISK?   68

HOW LONG WILL IT TAKE ME TO LEARN TO TRADE OPTIONS?   68

WHAT IF I DO NOT HAVE TIME TO LEARN HOW TO TRADE?   69

SO, HOW POSSIBLE IS TRADING OPTIONS FOR A LIVING? 69

CHAPTER FIVE – LIMITING YOUR DOWNSIDE WHILE TRADING TRENDS.......**71**

LEVERAGING ASSETS TO REDUCE RISK   71

DETERMINING YOUR TOTAL DOLLARS AT RISK   72

TRUSTING MARKET TIMING   77

COMBINING OPTIONS TO REDUCE RISK   81

SPREADING THE RISK WITH A DEBIT TRADE   83

HOW TO SPREAD THE RISK WITH A CREDIT TRADE   89

CHAPTER SIX – TARGETING SECTORS WITH TECHNICAL ANALYSIS 95

GETTING TECHNICAL WITH CHARTS   95

REGULATING YOUR TIME HORIZON FOR THE GREATEST VIEW   98

VISUALIZING SUPPLY AND DEMAND   99

IDENTIFYING RELATIVELY STRONG SECTORS   103

RATE OF CHANGE INDICATOR   107

USING SECTOR VOLATILITY TOOLS   108

ANALYZING VOLATILITY WITH BOLLINGER BANDS   112

PROJECTING PRICES FOR TRADING   114

SUPPORT AND RESISTANCE   115

TRENDS   117

CHANNELS 118

PROJECTIONS AND PROBABILITIES   124

CHAPTER SEVEN – GUARDING YOUR ASSETS WITH OPTIONS 128

PUTTING PROTECTION ON LONG STOCK   128

COMBINING PUTS WITH LONG STOCK   129

LIMITING THE RISK OF SHORT STOCK WITH CALLS   138

HEDGING YOUR BETS WITH OPTIONS   142

AVOIDING ADJUSTED OPTION RISK   150

ADJUSTING FROM ADJUSTMENTS 154

CHAPTER EIGHT – CAPITALIZING WHEN MARKET MOVES SIDEWAYS 158

WINNING POSITIONS IN SIDEWAYS MARKETS   158

MANAGE EXISTING POSITIONS   159

COMMENTS ON THE STRATEGY   159

DEFINING THE LONG BUTTERFLY 166

CHAPTER NINE - PASSIVE INCOME STRATEGY 171

PUT OPTIONS   172

GENERATE MONTHLY PROFITS WITH PUT OPTIONS   173

3

CALL OPTIONS 174

GENERATING MONTHLY PROFITS WITH CALL OPTIONS 174

COVERED-CALL STRATEGY175

Copyright © 2020

ABOUT THIS BOOK

There are a lot of trading titles out there, including those focused on option strategies. This book focuses primarily on risk management-approaches, the best options strategies, the consistent theme all through. By configuring it this way, you can approach different topics, keeping this main objective in mind. So, go ahead, go to the areas that interest you.

This book can be read from one end to the other or used as a reference guide. Each strategy provided identifies the risks and benefits associated with the position. It also identifies alternative strategies to consider in risk management, if any. There are millions of ways to succeed in trading markets, but some challenges are universal for all. Tools and techniques to address these challenges are also provided.

This book offers options strategies for managing risk and navigating various market conditions. I really believe in taking care of the risk first, the profits will follow. With this in mind, the approaches you find here focus on reducing the potential losses of traditional equity positions and creating a repertoire of option strategies that can make gains as the markets go up, down, or fall. To integrate the complete steps required during the negotiation, it also provides discussions on market and industry analysis, as well as elements to look for when trying out a new strategy.

OPTIONS TRADING 2021

CHAPTER ONE – OPTIONS TRADING 2021 AND INVESTMENT

Whether you're new to trading or that you are an experienced investor, the listed options on stocks and indices are excellent vehicles to manage risk and increase your assets. The wide diversity of strategies available using these titles makes them suitable for just about everyone - as long as you understand how they work and apply them correctly. I started trading options many years ago and found that by using different strategies, I could implement business profiles with reasonable risk-reward over the years.

Trade and investment are usually differentiated by deadlines. I believe that investing is something you accomplish to achieve long-term financial goals. Whatever plan you personally create to achieve these goals, the options provide a way to protect long-term assets during periods when markets face them.

Although I primarily use the term trading to invest or trade, I consider it to be a market approach to achieving superior returns to help build these investments over the long term. Higher yields mean taking additional risks, but I certainly want to say measured risks. At the very least, the approaches proposed in this book should reinforce the focus you need to keep on the risk, reward, and effective management of positions, no matter which financial asset you choose to use.

Trading times may be shorter, but do not get me wrong... I am not talking about hyperactive day-trading, where you are glued to your screen. Stock options and indices offer strategies that require day-to-day management, as well as those that can be reviewed weekly or more. It's up to you to implement the appropriate approaches to your risk tolerances and preferences, as well as your schedule.

UNDERSTANDING OPTIONS IN 2021

Options are financial tools that derive their value from another underlying asset or a financial measure - here, I focus on equities and market indices. Because options are in two forms, calls and calls, adding them to your current trading and trading tools allows you to benefit from up and down movements on the underlying movements you select. You can do this to limit the total assets at risk or to protect an existing position.

To truly understand the stock options and indices, you must also have a solid understanding of the asset on which they are based. It may mean looking differently at movements of stocks or indices - for example; volatility is an essential component of the value of the option. By comparing options with the underlying securities or other securities, your learning curve is directed towards their application.

The main purpose of trading any security is to understand its risks, including all of the following:

- Know the conditions to consider when analyzing a trade
- Use the right commercial mechanics when creating a job
- Recognize trading rules and requirements
- Understand what makes the position win and lose value

The following sections discuss these key options components to provide a good platform for creating rewarding positions.

KNOWING OPTION ESSENTIALS

A stock option listed is a two-party contractual agreement with standard terms. When you create a new position, buying an option gives you rights, and selling an option leaves you with obligations. These rights and obligations are guaranteed by Option Clearing Corporation (OCC), so you never have to worry about the trader is on the other side of the contract.

A major risk you face with options is the risk of time because contracts have a limited life. A call option becomes worthwhile when the underlying stock increases, but if the move is too late, the purchase may expire worthlessly. On the plus side, options have expiration dates ranging from 9 months to 21/2 years.

Your rights as an appellant include all of the following:

- Buy a specific amount of underlying shares
- Purchase until a certain date (expiry)
- Purchase at a specified price (called strike price)

This is why the purchase price increases when the stock price rises - the price you are entitled to is fixed when the stock itself increases in value.

A put option becomes valuable when your stock falls, but the timing is the same. The change must take place before the expiration of the option contract. Your sales contract rights include the sale of a specific quantity of stock before a certain date at a specified price. If you have the right to sell a stock for $ 60, but the bad news about the company lowers the price to $ 60, those rights become more valuable.

Acquiring skills as an options trader means selecting options with expiry dates that allow time for the intended moves to occur. This may seem very difficult at the moment, but some basic rules are helpful. These rules include good transaction management, which means leaving a position if it moves against you and reaches its predetermined exit point.

Each stock with options present has a variety of expiry dates and exercise prices. When searching for options, you will find the following:

- A longer time-out option is more expensive.
- An option with a lower exercise price is more expensive.

Information on all available options can be found on the Internet from various sources, including your broker. The selection of the best, given the current conditions and their point of view on the actions, takes a little time, but it's not rocket science. Your biggest problems are those associated with any type of negotiation: managing your own emotions and exercising discipline.

GETTING COMFORT WITH OPTION MECHANICS

Options differ from actions in terms of what they represent and how they are created. This results in additional rules for negotiation and decision-making beyond basic buying or selling considerations. You may decide to simply leave the position in the market or exercise your rights under the contract.

Are these additional complications worth it? For many people, yes. The differences in the mechanics of stocks and options are very simple and manageable. A big advantage of these securities is the way they provide leverage. By controlling share rights rather than the stocks themselves, you significantly reduce your risk.

From the beginning of this book, I have identified the factors that affect the value of an option, as well as the most appropriate conditions for buying and selling different contracts. By understanding how options provide leverage and reduce your trading risk, you begin to understand why I use the term risk initially measured.

RECOGNIZING RISKS AND REWARDS OF OPTIONS

The main risk associated with options is the risk of time. You have the tendency to lose your entire investment if the change you expect is too little or too late. It's not an all-or-nothing proposition for you. You may decide to exit an option position if an adverse movement occurs in the underlying stock before expiration. It all comes down to disciplined negotiations.

The valuation of equity risk versus call and put risk creates a strong foundation for understanding the risk and benefits created by more complex option positions. Visualizing these risks on a chart develops your ability to evaluate an option swap. The risk graphs, which represent the value of the position in relation to the price of the underlying stock, are a trading tool that will be valuable to you throughout your trading career.

INTEGRATE OPTIONS INTO YOUR ROUTINE

Understanding the options and what motivates their prices offers another view of the stock market. In addition to the sentiment information provided by options trading, the conditions that you must understand as an options trader can help your stock market analysis. These market features also help you analyze and select sectors to achieve your goals.

As with any new market approach or strategy, adding options to your trading means the following:

Understand the benefits and risks associated with them Test them safely or at low risk

Options can be "tested" by monitoring price changes, using paper trading strategies, and focusing on a limited number of strategies adapted to current conditions. In addition to these steps, it allows you to take into account the negotiation costs associated with this security.

ADDING OPTIONS TO YOUR ANALYSIS

The analysis of trading options can easily integrate with your current market analysis, complementing it with sentiment tools. Market-wide tools and sentiment analysis often focus on extreme conditions to identify periods when there is the greatest potential for market reversals. Basically, when the last trader gets short, it's a bullish signal for the future. Optional measures that help recognize extreme conditions include contract volume and implied volatility readings for key market indices. So, by adding sentiment analysis to an amplitude analysis, you get a nice confirmation of pending changes.

The options analysis focuses on two aspects of the market:

- Trend conditions
- Volatility conditions

Although stock traders are also aware of trend conditions, they may be less in line with volatility conditions. Or perhaps there is a strong emotional feeling of greater volatility, but not quantitative.

A technical analysis designed to provide insight into trends and volatility helps you focus on stock options or trading. Adding information to the industry analysis allows you to use underlying groups that behave differently to diversify your holdings better and spread your risk. The combination of industry analysis and options also offers good low-risk alternatives for capitalizing downside movements through the use of put options.

TRYING OUT INVESTING AND TRADING STRATEGIES

Option values are not based solely on the price of the underlying stock you are trading. Other factors affect the market price of an option. Reading these other factors is a good start, but to better understand price dynamics before you have money at stake, you can take other steps.

There are various techniques at your disposal designed to provide the following:

> • A better intuitive understanding of changes in the underlying stocks (and the market in general) that affect the price of an option.
> • Practical knowledge of simulation mechanics

Therefore, becoming proficient in option strategies requires practicing through paper trading - similar to stock trading. But before that, you really need to understand how real market changes affect the values of options over time. Once you have done this, you can get a lot more from the paper exchange. You can concentrate on other trading costs, including slip and margin requirements, as well as ways to better execute trades.

Paper trading is not the only method you can borrow from stock trading to look into a new strategy. Back - Testing an option approach may take a little longer than a stock approach, but it could certainly save you a lot of money. By having a plan that slows you down to face different nuances of trading options in advance, you will define disciplined trading skills.

PUTTING OPTIONS TO WORK

option contracts can be used for financial tools or hedge for speculating. When buying an option contract, you are able to exercise your rights or simply trade away the rights. Needs and conditions dictate different art. You want to be prepared to assess the situation and do what is best. Exercising an option to minimize stock market risk is just one way for you to put the options at your service.

Reasonably minimizing risk is the name of the investment game, so it is very useful to know how to protect existing positions and strategies by adding options. The hedge can be implemented position by position or covering the entire portfolio. If instead of a short-term bearish outlook that requires protection, your opinion becomes so negative that you are looking for downside trading opportunities, the options offer a much safer approach than selling an action or a short-term sector.

Another way for options to make big efforts for your investments is to use leverage. By spending less on the initial investment, you are responding to a reduced risk approach, but that does not mean you should get reduced returns. Basic strategies can help you accomplish both. And if speculation is part of your modus operandi, you can risk even less when you are ready to limit your profits.

UNDERSTANDING THE OPTION STYLES

There is a major focus on stock options in this book, but it's hard to ignore another important segment of the stock market. This is the index market. The striking difference between a stock and an index is that the stock is a tradable stock. An index can not. This means that the exercise of the index option takes on a new dimension. Since this is not the only difference between the two types of options, it is important to understand how your rights and transactions are affected by the option style you choose to use.

USING OPTIONS TO LIMIT YOUR RISKS

Comparing the risk profiles of stocks and options is a good start to appreciate the value that options bring to your investments, but the use of strategies to capitalize on these stocks is much better. Assessing the many protection options available is one of the first steps in implementing all strategies. Spend some time understanding why some will better serve their goals than others will turn theoretical discussions into real applications:

The risk for an existing position: The risk for existing positions can be reduced to varying degrees, ranging from reasonable protection to full hedges, adjusted to market conditions.

The risk for a new position: The risk for new positions can be reduced similarly to a very little amount using a combination of options or less significantly with unique long-term options.

Account approvals for strategies that make use of long options combined with stocks or individually are usually available for most traders. As you acquire experience and have more strategies, you can actually customize a position risk profile using combinations of options. This includes:

- Vertical debit spreads
- Vertical credit spreads
- Calendar Spreads
- Diagonal differences

Access to different strategies involves implementing approaches that are best suited to existing market conditions.

APPLICATION OF OPTIONS TO SECTORAL APPROACHES

ETFs can be one of the most effective investment products introduced in decades. They offer great diversification, like mutual funds (MF), but far surpass both areas:

Ability to leave an ETF as needed with a quoted market price during the day (not when calculating the value at the end of the day)

EXISTENCE OF OPTIONS USING ETFS AS SECURITY

Needless to say, I really like this second. Portfolios can be built using ETFs and ETF options for protection or making use of ETF options for the entire portfolio.

USING OPTIONS IN DIFFICULT MARKETS

Equities and ETFs offer a great way to participate in bull or bear markets, but there is still a third potential price trend - which is lateral. By adding strategies that let you capitalize on this third trend alternative, you are taking a step further to allow the market to dictate your approach.

In addition to responding to a third potential market trend, option strategies allow you to reduce directional risk by taking advantage of upward or downward movements rather than one direction. You can create a combined position and adjust it over time as prices change. This approach responds to market movements rather than trying to predict.

REDUCING YOUR DIRECTIONAL BIAS

Stock positions, long or short, have a directional bias as they depend on movement in one direction for profit. Options allow you to minimize directional bias by creating combined positions that can be profitable if the underlying moves up or down.

Therefore, not only can you better control maximum losses with options, but you can also reduce directional risk by using strategies that can be achieved with two of three possible directional motions. These approaches are based on neutral delta trading styles, which introduce a new way of thinking about the market.

BENEFITTING WHEN MARKETS ARE EVERYWHERE

A stock can remain in a lateral trend channel for an extended period, offering option traders a way to take advantage when most traders can not. Although the lateral model may be long-term, the option strategies that take advantage of it are shorter in nature. These extended models also tend to cause strong movements away from the recessed channel and generally test the model before continuing. This prepares you for a change of strategy from the beginning of a new trend.

CONSIDERING YOUR OBSTACLES

Whether you trade stocks, ETFs, currencies, or options, there are similar obstacles to success that need to be overcome. The main thing is your makeup. Negotiation evokes certain emotions that can wreak havoc on your bottom line unless you actively manage it.

You might consider exciting new trading strategies, but be careful when you jump the weapon. Good preparation is required. Three steps to follow before using a new marketing strategy:

- Understand the risks and rewards of security
- Practice Strategies
- Analyze a trade

Although this book covers many topics of "learning" and "analysis," this chapter presents tools and techniques for practicing strategies. First, by monitoring the different options pricing components and paper trading, you simulate the actual conditions. This gives you a more intuitive feel for price changes and helps you avoid costly mistakes. Then, by developing your backtest prowess, you implement only the greatest approaches, allowing you to stay long enough in the game to gain valuable experience. Through experience and practice, you finally achieve mastery of the strategy.

MONITORING OPTION GREEK CHANGES

Understanding basic option strategies is a much faster learning curve than recognizing the right price for options used in strategies. But among the most effective techniques to really understand the value of these bonds is to monitor the price and the Greek changes in conditions. real.

TRACKING PREMIUM MEASURES

Developing your skills with any option strategy really means understanding how option grants are affected by changes in the following:

- The price of the underlying
- Expiration time

A great method to get a better intuitive feel for their impact is to track daily changes in all the different components. All you have to do is access market prices, an options calculator, and a spreadsheet. By taking note of a few different options, you should learn a lot about how changing conditions affect prices in general. By including the Greeks in the process, you also understand what factors play the most important roles at different times.

Ideally, you will end up reviewing the markets and monitoring prices over a period when prices move a little. This makes it possible to highlight the delta, gamma, and theta impacts on the price. Before putting your money at risk, set up a spreadsheet to track the following:

- Price of underlying

- Price for calls ITM, ATM, OTM
and e foreshore maturity ed variables
- Days before expiration
- Intrinsic value option, delta, gamma and theta

By following these values, you can identify the metrics that have the greatest impact on option strategies.

The delta can be displayed on the basis of values from -1 to +1 or from -100 to +100.

CHANGING VOLATILITY AND OPTION PRICES

The impact of volatility on option prices is sometimes somewhat difficult to understand because implied volatility (IV) includes price factors that vary over the life of the option. IV includes the following elements:

- Past volatility (historical)
- Expected future volatility (implicit) and
- Request for a contract

Past volatility

Crowd behavior can inflate option prices when demand for some contracts increases as news of a company arrives.

Implied volatility (IV)

Implied volatility (IV) is the implied volatility of the option price. Does this cover everything for you? Given that the IV is a very important option price factor, it is probably a good idea to expand this definition a bit.

In terms of trading and IV:

- It is best to buy options when the IV is relatively low.
- It is better to sell options when the IV is relatively high.

The problem with these basic rules is that you can not always follow them. By maintaining a long-term ownership position, you want to protect; you just have to throw caution in the wind, and put IV high? Certainly not, especially considering that increasing the IV often results in a growing fear in the market. When you are faced with call options in a highly volatile environment, you may need to evaluate a wider range of months to maturity and strike prices.

When the implied volatility (IV) is relatively high, then it decreases considerably, it is called IV crush.

Remember that IV can vary:

- Until maturity, which contributes to more uncertainty about the value of the option.
- For the exercise price: Usually, the cashier IV (ATM) is the lowest, but it does not always work that way. Asymmetric charts provide IV at the strike price and can speed up the process of selecting options when you have to buy contracts, while IV is relatively high. An option price can be divided into two components: the intrinsic and extrinsic value. The value is entirely determined by the value of the option, but IV does not play any role in this value. The deeper the option (ITM), the lower the IV will have an impact on the total price of the option.

By using short option strategies, time reduction works in your favor. Trading options with 30 to 45 days to expire accelerates this deterioration for you.

PAPER TRADING AN APPROACH

The pursuit and implementation of new strategies naturally develop your trading skills. With paper trading, you can move safely in the new strategic learning curve.

When trading on paper, be sure to incorporate the trading costs associated with the position to get the best value for the profitability of the strategy.

Paper trading: advantages and disadvantages

Paper trading is a great way to minimize losses by learning the mechanics of the strategy or by slightly modifying your trading routine. Looking at a long money-out option (OTM) decreasing the value as the implied volatility decreases is much less painful when it's on paper. However, it does not really prepare you for the battle of greed and fear inside. However, this forces you to face it before you have money online.

Establishment of electronic paper exchanges

The paper exchange can be done in a spreadsheet, electronic platform or... You have it, paper. Do what's best for you If you plan to create your own diary, also include the Greek option.

Many financial sites allow you to enter different positions in a portfolio tracker that is updated late in the day or late in the day. Unfortunately, not everyone accepts option symbols. A basic tracker will give position information that includes price changes with the result. A more advanced platform may include displays of risk charts and other transaction management tools.

USE OF TRADING SYSTEMS

A trading system is a tactic with precise rules of entry and exit. Even if you are currently using a systematic approach to a strategy - that is, you only buy a call when the implied volatility is relatively low - a trading system is more narrowly defined. When using a system, you must do the following:

Set a position for all purchase signals generated by the rules Exit each position when the output signal is generated

Know what you get

There is no decision making when implementing the system - you never think about accepting an input or output signal. If you accumulate losses or something seems wrong, you shut down the system completely. The two greatest things about a formal system are:

- It minimizes your trade emotions
- It allows backtests to get an idea of expected performance.

If you start to exercise discretion in deciding what to do, these two benefits will disappear. Emotions appear, and their results may differ considerably from test results. As with any trading strategies, an essential key to system trading is working with systems that are tailored to your trading style and the size of your account.

Although the rules of a system are strict, flexibility is common by varying the speed of the indicators or by adding filters. A filter is an additional rule for exchanging inputs or outputs. Indicators and comparable system components are defined as system parameters.

The characteristics of a good trading system include:

- Profitability in various markets, securities, and market conditions
- Overcoming a purchase and maintenance approach
- Stability with manageable drawdowns
- Diversify your trading tools
- Adapted to your style and the availability of your time

Be extremely careful when designing a system and put it on the autopilot. Always watch the negotiations.

PERFORMING A BACKTEST

A backtest uses historical data to determine whether a system generates stable earnings. You can perform backtests using data downloads or mechanical transaction tracking, but the most efficient way to do this is to use a software application for backtests. You just have to make sure you test what you think you are testing.

When backtesting a system, include longer periods to capture bullish, bearish, and lateral markets. In this way, you get results in the worst conditions and experience (in a test environment) realistic downshifts. Drawdown is the term used to define accumulated losses on accounts resulting from consecutive loss transactions. Evaluating lifting is just another way of managing a man and his risk.

A robust trading system works for a lot of markets (stocks, commodities, etc.) under a variety of conditions (bull and bear markets).

By examining the results of the backtests, you are looking for profitability and stability. Stability refers to the consistency of the results - you want to know if only a few operations generate all the profits or are spread over a variety of operations. A stable system:

- It has winning deals with average profits that exceed the average losses of lost trades.
- At an average system benefit close to the median system benefit (low standard deviation)
- Suspends manageable samples
- Do not trust some profitability trades

Note that a system does not need to have more winning operations than losing trades. Many trend systems rely on the ability to run profits for fewer transactions while quickly reducing losses on lost trades.

After creating a system with reasonable backtest performance, you perform advanced tests by running the rules in a shorter time. Typically, you start the test on the last backtest date and run at some point before implementation. Expect diminishing returns in advanced tests. System trading is not an undisclosed key that generates profits. It is a way of minimizing harmful professional emotions. Consider this approach that deserves your attention if you're ready to roll up your sleeves and explore.

Following the right steps

Follow these steps when re-testing a system:
- Identify the basis of the strategy (i.e., enter trend conditions).
- Identify incoming and outgoing trading rules.
- Identify the negotiated market and the backtest of the period.
- Identify the assumptions of account (system and commercial allocations).
- Test system; evaluate the results.
- Identify the reasonable filters to minimize the loss of trades (number and / or size of these trades)

- Add a filter based on the results from step 6; test system; then evaluate the results.
- Add a risk management component.
- Test system; evaluate the results.

Check the average value of the trading loss as well as the maximum and consecutive losses to determine if a system is suitable.

System time as the rate of change (ROC) was tested by using a simple displacement cross means (ADM) for signaling the entry of the trade [ROC 34 SMA: 13] and output [ROC 21 SMA: 8]. As a faster signal was used for the release of the trade, a second parameter had to be added to the trade entry, requiring that the 21-day ROC be greater than its 13-day SMA. Otherwise, the appropriate commercial output may never be reported. It is a trend system that seeks to capitalize on a long-term upward momentum. To limit profit losses and erosion, a faster moment signal is used to exit the position.

The backtest was conducted over a six-year period that included periods of highs and lows (1999-2005) in a group of six semiconductor stocks, including SMH, an ETF for the sector. US $ 20,000 was used for the system, with 50% of the money available used for each bargaining. $ 10 per sales commission has been added to the costs. No stops were part of the initial test of the system.

A system need not be robust to be effective. Since volatility and trend characteristics vary for different securities, some are better suited to certain types of systems.

Review of system results

Risk management is the main theme of this book; evaluating a non-stop system may seem counterintuitive. However, when you think about it, stop levels are pretty arbitrary - the market really does not care if you enter a $ 45 position. It may or may not be supported at 5% or 10% below. Allow the system to recognize a viable stop-loss point by retesting it and decide if it presents an appropriate risk to you.

The results of the system have been very favorable in many measurements for the initial execution, so no filter has been added. The maximum adverse excursion percentage was revised to determine if a reasonable stop level could be added. A 15% downtime was added, and the system test was run again. The results were just a little less favorable, so the parade was incorporated.

Graphics packages can use different calculations for the same indicator. If you change systems, compare the values of the indicators that provide signals to exchange the same system being tested. Always think about retesting the system on the new platform.

Two advanced tests were also performed, with and without stopping. Both - periods of the year were used for each, and the system remained viable with much lower profitability. Expect this to happen with actual system performance and advanced tests. This is due to changing inefficiencies and conditions that are developed from the markets. It's one of the reasons why you need to review the performance of the system periodically and integrate reasonable stops whenever positive.

A lower percentage stop can be considered as an approximation of average and median returns, but since average incomes are greater than average losses (allowing profits to work), you must first compare the mean and median to earn and lose. business separately.

You can make use of a standard deviation evaluation to evaluate profit stability for any market approach.

ADDING RISK MANAGEMENT TO A BACKTEST

All business approaches must consider risk management. Put the emphasis on the largest adverse movements for a strategy trying to identify cases that still allow the working strategy. If adding this downtime maintains cost-effectiveness and system stability, and fits your risk tolerance, consider implementing the strategy or system.

Cutting losses

A systematic but non-mechanical approach can still be tested. Regardless of how you perform this backtest, you should keep an eye on the major adverse moves that have occurred in the generated transactions. This allows you to identify reasonable filters and systematic stops designed to minimize losses.

A stop-loss order can result in a higher loss percentage when a transaction is executed. The worst case occurs when a signal is generated at the close of trading one day, and the security shows a price difference on opening the next day.

Taking profits

Identify risk-loss stopping points that are probably already second-hand. On the other side of this, have you ever been to a lucrative business that is starting to move in the wrong direction? At this point, you realize that you do not have a specific exit plan to make a profit. Sometimes you focus so much on the risk that you forget to identify the target prices favorable. Or you may have identified a lucrative exit point, but conditions begin to deteriorate before that price level is reached.

In addition to identifying a stop loss level, identifying a stop percentage or a dollar value to minimize the number of profitable transactions that turn into losses. The trailing stop should be built into your system, or the strategy is the strategy and tested. If you had like the system to generate the trailing value, consider trading with large moves that are favorable that earned much less in terms of profits (or transformed into losses). After completing your exam, you can do the following:

- Add a filter that speeds up your trips
- Generate a percentage right using the most favorable tour data

Letting the benefits run

An effective business approach does not have to have more gains than transaction losses. It only needs profits to overcome declines. This is indeed the case for many trend-oriented platforms. You end up with additional losing trades, but the average value of the loss is well below the average value of the trades. And so , go the mantra, "Make sure you reduce your losses while letting the profits run."

Sorting the highest loss or profit transactions makes it easier to see the statistics for both.

Although you need to identify a method to make a profit, you should also avoid lowering profit levels so that they no longer make up for losses. Successful trading requires a little pre-work. You will see your trading evolve, focusing on the following points:

- Reduce losses.
- Prevent profits from turning into losses.
- Leaving the profits running.

SHIFTING FROM KNOWLEDGE TO MASTERY

Controlling strategy does not mean that all the transactions you perform for a given strategy are profitable - it means that the right conditions were in place when executing a particular transaction, placing the odds in your favor for a particular strategy. profitable operation. Proper management of the position is also another element that highlights discipline when leaving a trade if conditions change. It sounds very easy, but mastering the strategy can take years to evolve. Your objective is to stay in the trading game long enough to reach this area.

By focusing first on the basics and mechanics, you create a solid foundation that allows you to understand advanced techniques more quickly. You implement new strategies through paper trading to avoid the most costly mistakes. When you're ready to announce the new strategy, you can further minimize the cost of errors by reducing the size of your position and remembering to make a profit. This approach allows you to stay in business longer, allowing you to find and develop strategies that best fit your style.

SETTING THE RIGHT PACE

There are a number of good choice strategies in this book, some of which are likely to pique your interest more than others. Start by negotiating some of the simplest approaches on paper, then go on to negotiate with them. After that, discover the strategy you prefer, again by the paper trade. There is no guarantee that the market conditions are favorable to this strategy is the strategy; Therefore, you may prolong your days of paper trading until the market changes or you are ready to explore a new strategy. But, It is really important to keep this in mind. You want to put the focus on the strategies that have meaning to you and agree the best for your style. This is how you will finally develop the domain.

Starting with some strategies

I hope that learning new strategies will please you. It's amazing to discover all the different ways to make money in the markets. But not all strategies and tactics work in all market conditions. More importantly, they will not all fit your style. If you are new to options trading, follow one or two basic strategies to develop a good understanding of change and premium mechanics.

There are a variety of strategies at your disposal that allow you to make money in the markets. In addition to your preferred method of analysis, you will find that you are developing a preferred list of strategies that favors you.

Experienced option traders must recognize current market conditions and then explore one, perhaps two, exceptional strategies considering these conditions. Start trading with paper and progress from there. If there is a specific strategy that really intrigues you or speaks to you, but the conditions are not good, just change it to paper. In the long run, it's best to focus on the market approaches that are right for you.

Adding strategies as market conditions change

I see markets as a permanent pursuit because conditions are always changing. Although there is a continuous cycle of ups and downs, the market is never exactly the same. It seems that you have already recognized it by buying the book first.

When the strategies that generally work well for you are starting to weaken, take the time during the weekend to perform a full market assessment. You can detect the first signs of a change in conditions.

Option trading lets you implement strategies that can be profitable regardless of market conditions. A sample includes:

- Low volatility (long base call, married sex)
- High and high volatility
- Low, low volatility (base selling, debit spreads
- Low and high volatility (collars, credit spreads
- Low volatility, limited by range
(butterfly, condor) The combination of stocks with options or options with options offers really great options. This can be bad or good news, as each approach takes time to master. Be careful when checking a strategy at random. rejecting it because it "does not work."

It is likely that you will not trade all available strategies. Most traders experiment differently along the way and then master a smaller number. The experience gained allows you to maximize profits on your favorite strategies (knowing when to keep them) while minimizing your losses (knowing when to double them).

Deciding which option strategies to use is like a market analysis - there are many ways to approach it, none of which is the "right" way. The best tactic for you is the one that makes the most sense intuitively, so when conditions change and things get harder (and better), you'll have the confidence to stick to your plan.

REALIZE MASTERY THROUGH LONGEVITY

The experience of different markets and the exploration of appropriate strategies require longevity in the markets. Rising markets may run for years, and volatile conditions may also remain stable. Expect additional losses when markets transition or when implementing a new strategy. Risk management using limited loss and unlimited gain strategies, to the extent possible, lays the foundation for longevity.

Paper switching provides a technique for minimizing learning curve losses. A second method is to size the position correctly. Starting with smaller starting positions, the potential losses are manageable. Adding rules that include making a profit is the icing on the cake.

Successful trading will never happen overnight. Be prepared to observe different market conditions, spend time making low-cost mistakes, feeling different levels of emotion, and developing your business skills.

Determination of appropriate business sizes

There are different techniques for identifying appropriate commercial sizes. Many go beyond the scope of this book simply because of space constraints. Two easily embeddable are:

- Identification of a maximum amount allocated per transaction
- Identification of a maximum percentage amount allocated per transaction

I prefer it because it changes automatically depending on the size of your account.

The options represent a leveraged position, so you do not have to allocate the same value to the option positions as for the stocks. In fact, it's probably not the best idea to do it. Using your stock allocation plan as a basis, you can estimate an initial allocation value by recognizing an option position that controls a similar amount of stock. This is a starting point that should be tested and revised.

Establish trade allocation values before analyzing a specific trade. You must know in advance the maximum amount available for an individual exchange to minimize the risk of your account.

When you try a new policy (after changing roles), further reduce the size of the transactions so that the errors are more tolerant. If it means negotiating the size of an option's contracts, so be it. Remember, you're not here to impress Wall Street with the size of your business - you're here to make money in the markets.

As your skills grow, increase the size of the positions for the tested allowances. This will increase profits as option trading costs are generally higher than the percentage of trading costs. If you have been well prepared and continue to manage your risks, increasing the size of the positions should not be a problem. In fact, this should improve results because you will get economies of scale with transaction costs.

Focusing on profit

Throughout this book, the focus is on risk management. In this chapter, however, there is an added emphasis - making a profit. It is not enough just to have a large number of lucrative businesses. Your profits must include the following:

- Exceed trading costs
- Exceeds prudent investment approaches
- Exceed your losses

This is not just for nothing; you must have a plan that includes a review of the strategy and business results to implement the best rules of profitability. These rules should minimize the number of profitable transactions that turn into losses and make profits. Developing these skills means that you evolve as a trader.

There are many different prices that can provoke an emotional response during a negotiation. Make sure to identify exit points for a loss and exit points for profits.

CHAPTER THREE – TOP TEN OPTION STRATEGIES

Trade is partly art, partly science. The development of rules and specific steps to be part of a process that puts you on the path to skillful trading. Implementing them with a focus on risk management gives you the time to develop your business. A great first step on the scientific side is to create a list of strategies. This lets you methodically approach a new type of trading to gain as much knowledge and experience as possible.

To begin, I wanted to provide a list of ten major option strategies. The common point with these strategies is that they have limited risk and are alternatives to consider. The unlimited or limited but high risk - risk strategies that could potentially replace are provided with the summary strategy.

Each of the top ten strategies includes:

- Name and components of the strategy
- Risks and rewards
- Optimal market conditions (trends, volatility)
- Advantages and disadvantages
- Basic risk profiles
- Additional information by strategy

By all means, think of adding notes to make them yours.

MARRIED PUT

A married put combines a long stock with a long put for protection. The position is created by buying shares and placing them at the same time, but the key is to create protection against sales. The purchase of a put option for existing shares or the launch of an option for a subsequent expiration month is consistent with this strategic objective. Long Out-of-Cash (OTM) options must be sold 30 to 45 days prior to expiration.

COLLAR

A collar combines a long stock with long-term protection and a short call reducing the cost of protection. An ideal scenario is when you can buy long-term stock and the call option in conditions of low volatility, allowing long-term protection. Calls are sold as volatility increases, and the expiration time is 30 to 45 days, so time decay accelerates short call gains.

LONG PUT TRADER

A long put is a low-risk limited position that wins when the underlying falls. This replaces a short position of unlimited risk stock that requires the establishment of more capital. The downward movement must occur when the option expires, and non-cash sales (OTM) must be discontinued 30 to 45 days prior to expiration.

LEAPS CALL INVESTOR

Long-term Equity Anticipation Security (LEAPS) reduces the costs and risks associated with a long stock position. The position is better established when the implied volatility is relatively low. The owner of LEAPS will not participate in dividend distributions that reduce the value of the shares.

DIAGONAL SPREAD

A diagonal gap combines an option from next month's short with a month's long option of the same type. When the exercise prices are the same, we talk about calendar spread. A short-term, neutral view can sell the short option to offset the costs of the long option. A diagonal call is described here, but a sales diagonal works as well when you are short-term in the long run.

CREDIT PROPAGATION BEAR CALL

A bearish spread combines a short and short strike price purchase with a longer and higher purchase ending in the same month. Create a credit and replace a short call with unlimited risk. It is best applied when implied volatility is high and 30 or 45 days or less before expiration.

STRADDLE

A straddle combines a long purchase with a long sale, using the same exercise expiration and price. It is built when volatility is low and should rise and win when prices rise or fall sharply. Since there are two long options, exit from the expiry position of 30 to 45 days to avoid a deterioration of time.

CALL RATIO BACKSPREAD

A call ratio backspread combines longer exercise prices for calls and higher with a lower number of lower strike calls that expire in the same month. It is best to implement it for a credit, and it is a potentially unlimited reward position with a limited risk that is more profitable when a bullish movement occurs.

LONG PUT BUTTERFLY

A long-selling butterfly combines a bull put spread, and a bear selling spread expiring in the same month for a debit. The two short positions have the same exercise price and make up the body. The two long positions have different exercise prices (above and below the body) and make up the wings. Deteriorating weather conditions contribute to trade.

TEN DOS AND DON'TS IN OPTION TRADING

Trade is partly art, partly science. Development as a trader begins with the use of a formula approach for different markets and strategies. The skillful application of an experienced professional requires practice, patience, and experience. It is a trip that you receive ideally.

I hope this book contains many rules, steps, and concrete methods. I sincerely hope this has also provided you with some important nuances of trading. Things that can not be applied mechanically. This seems to be the perfect point to focus on those who are here.

Do Focus on Managing Risk

The game is known as risk management. In fact, when people ask you what you do and what you do, say that you are a risk manager. Become one with him. Now, if it's not nuanced, I do not know what it is.

By exploring only option strategies, you are actively addressing other financial risks in your life. This includes the risk of inflation, income risk, and even the market risk associated with buying and maintaining the investment.

When your trading is based on risk management, you:

- Understand the risks and benefits associated with the markets in which you trade. Learn and test strategies before putting money at risk.
- Create a plan that identifies the entry and exit approaches of the enterprise size and the maximum allowable loss. Be aware of how the plan will be implemented to meet your risk parameters.
- Understand how to manage trade and establish positions.
- Have a plan to make a profit
- Ask yourself, "What if I'm wrong?

Other more general risk considerations include sector diversification and negotiated strategies. You can correctly allocate trading sizes, but if you enter five trend trades using the same strategy on stocks in the same sector, you are going against this trading size rule. That's the nuance. By extending these portfolio-based guidelines, you are acting more like an effective risk manager.

Don't Avoid Losses

In one way or the other, you will have losses in your trades. This is not a feature for beginners; It's just a cost to do business. In fact, suffering small losses is a skill developed by experienced traders. Try to reach this level sooner or later.

Avoiding losses is one way to increase them. You can make use of your rules and see positive results with a series of small wins and losses, just to clear the board (then some) with a big loss. This is a discouraging setback.

By shifting your vision of what constitutes successful trading from one profit to another following its rules, you are on the road to true success. Initially, you can tell yourself to do it, but you often become a true believer with experience. When this happens, you become more involved in a rules-based approach, and that's when change happens.

Do Trade with Discipline

Disciplined trade means following your rules in every trade. Not in part or most of the time, but always. Will you have a perfect record in front of the discipline? Probably not. . . Somewhere along the line, your human feelings will improve you. If you do not have the discipline at the beginning, and you have the chance to stay in the commercial game, your best discipline   is continually improving. Otherwise,   it only takes a short period of time before your luck runs out.

Unfortunately, those who have been successful initially can delay the appreciation and commitment to disciplined negotiation. Initial success can give you a false sense of being right, and that's not the point.

The characteristics of a disciplined trade in each trade are as follows:

- Allocate a reasonable amount to an operation
- Identify a maximum business risk
- Identification of input and output signals
- Run an order when your plan requires it

These are the elements of the checklist, but the disciplined trade goes beyond that. Do your homework, review your business, evaluate your plan. . . I do not think I could create a complete list. It's about learning what you need to do to negotiate successfully, mapping out how you're going to do it, and putting it into practice.

Don't wait to withdraw your emotions

Some traders assume that successfully trading means completely defeating your greed and your emotions of fear. I am here to tell you that that day means that you will have no emotion. . . It is certainly not a good thing. Eliminating emotions when negotiating is not a reasonable goal; However, their management is.

Things that can trigger emotions include:

- Negotiate using a discretionary approach
- Make business decisions when markets are open
- Use a stock or an underlying sector that owes you a transaction due to past losses

The ways to deal with these specific elements include:

- Focus on more systematic approaches
- Identification of non-worked hours for examination and management of operations
- Move away from a specific stock or industry, even if you generally trade successfully

There are even times when not negotiating for a certain period is the best way to adjust your attitude and your approaches.

Tracking your emotions is the first step in their management. Remember to add a note to your business records to follow them. Also, watch your emotions outside business hours. . . if you wake up grumpy or worse, can not sleep at night, your emotions control you.

Do Have a Plan

Many Wall Street statements have been around for quite some time, as they simply stay loyal to graduates year after year. Other sayings also include one that fits perfectly here: "When you do not plan, you plan to fail."

The creation of a baseline must certainly be considered a process and not a one-off event. Think of the "draft" and start by writing a plan. Completing it with a word-processing document or an easily editable spreadsheet can be great, but if you feel like you're on too much computer, a good old paper and pen are fine. The obsolete approach allows you to take notes along the way without hesitation because the computer is off. The essential thing is to create something.

When carrying out your first trading plan, set a deadline for completion and return three months later. This gives you a chance to throw the wheels, identify what seems to work and not work. It also highlights the elements that may be missing. Schedule a second review about six months later, then set a regular schedule that makes sense.

In addition to key risk management elements, start incorporating items such as general rules (for example, buying weak implicit options and selling high default options where possible) and the steps you will take to do so (for example, review historical and implied volatility graphs and verification of implied volatility levels with an options calculator).

Identifying other aspects of your trading work also helps (for example, analyzing market situations for long-term investments discretely from short-term trading) and again how you will get there (e.g., monthly Saturday analysis investments, Sunday Weekly Analysis for Negotiations).

As markets and your personal circumstances change over time, expect your trading plan to change as well. Better yet, plan it.

Do Be Patient

Because the focus is on risk management and creating a plan, you can feel a lot of pressure to create the "right" plan. Try to understand that there is almost always more at stake when there is no plan, as opposed to a plan that requires some work.

Part of the trading plan process includes adjusting your rules. This is certainly something you do outside of office hours, and that is the result of evaluating the strategy's performance and working to improve your overall trading plan. This can mean an increase in trading allocations or stop loss percentages or trading fewer strategies at the same time.

Your plan can be very aggressive or very conservative, but at least it serves as a basis for adjustments. Sketching two will be better? Probably, but market conditions can affect the effectiveness of your adjustments. Okay; At a particular time, you will have traded in a variety of conditions and learned techniques to take advantage of them. This is called experience and takes time.

Patience is not just for trading plans. Sometimes the best thing a professional can do is nothing. . . Waiting for trading or expecting profits are valuable skills that can have a big impact on trading profitability.

Don't undergo analysis for paralysis

If you like to play with the numbers, the economy and the financial markets provide an infinite number. You could probably spend years looking for relationships between different metrics, trying to get market timing signals. Then you can backtest and test in advance all the existing indicators to see which ones give you the ideal trading signals.

The paper business all the time will not necessarily bring you closer to a successful business. At a particular point in time, you will need to know the markets where you, the human trader, will react differently when trading live.

As mentioned, part of trading is managing your emotions and not deleting them. There is another aspect of that because there are also great emotions and characteristics that you bring to the table. Trust becomes so important when the market image begins to fade - that's what makes you follow your reasonably proven rules.

Therefore, the market with all your data can provide interesting diversions, but it keeps you from the task at hand. After all their learning, exam, testing, the practice, and analysis are made to a policy, in taking the experience provides live solidifying their understanding of everything. If this is your first trading option, use limited risk strategies and appropriate trading sizes to gain this experience. And if all goes well, you will also earn money along the way.

Take responsibility for your results

Never change the responsibility for your business results to anyone or to yourself. Why put your success in the hands of someone else? This makes it very elusive.

Throughout your trading career, certain situations or issues that affect the profitability of the business will surely arise. If there is a problem with executions, think about how you order and discuss it with your broker. If problems persist, correct them by transferring some of your assets to another broker and measure those results.

When you only have limited time for your standard exam due to work restrictions, personal appointments. . . Anyway, move on to strategies that you have time to do the right way. If there is still not enough time, getting away from trading is your only responsible option. Do not worry; the markets will always be there when you can reach them. And when you do, you will have kept some assets for trading.

Always recognizing that you are responsible for your own results, you seek solutions faster and take control. No need to wait for another person to take action or an event to happen. Doing this at the beginning of the game makes it possible to assert a much wider command on your learning curve and accelerates successful negotiations.

Do not stop learning

The changing nature of markets makes it almost impossible to avoid this. Since the economic conditions, the ups and downs of the market, and international markets are never exactly repeated, there is always the possibility of learning.

There are a variety of analytical tactics for trading, and each has a greater variety of techniques and tools to explore. Add to the mix new products introduced periodically, and you will have your work ready for you.

It may seem that there is a contradictory message here; I suggested focusing on some strategies rather than adopting a variety of different approaches. The objective was the control of the strategy and remains important. However, when you are on this path, a manageable number of new strategies must be explored. Market conditions dictate it simply.

It is useful to have a game plan for continuing education. . . especially if you want to have a good relationship with your friends, family, colleagues, etc. (also known as balance in your life). Here are some quick opinions to help you create yours:

By mastering the strategies, you will find topics that you want to understand better. Address these questions in a targeted way through self-study (books, CDs, periodicals).

Move to other forms and analysis strategies through more formal education if needed (live classes or DVDs, book manuals) or self-study.

Start the year with general objectives (for example, learn two strategies and more about technical analysis), as well as more details (for example, find strategies that benefit from markets with lateral tendency, better understand -markets).

Many traders naturally continue to learn as they turn to books, articles, news programs, conversations. . . deal with the markets. This is a perfect introduction to my last comment on what, in my opinion, is essential to your success in the negotiations.

I love the game

As with many other traders, I like to read about markets, trade, and other traders. As I check the discussions about the characteristics of successful traders, I often see "love the game." Believe me

The key factors for successful traders really include the challenge of understanding the markets, applying the right approach, and being disciplined. It's not about linking them or making money for them. This is partly because you have to love something that requires such intense work - not necessarily long hours but certainly focused. And in terms of money, this single-engine will eventually lead to big losses for most traders. The long and practiced path for all others must be appreciated.

There is a chance that you think you understand what I mean, but I feel that you know exactly what I mean. Be passionate about your trading, and accept your challenge. There is a healthy excitement about this activity that you have chosen throughout your life.

Is it possible to trade options for a living? That's what everyone wants to know.

It seems that everyone hates his work and wants to relax and exchange options for a few minutes a day and get a very good income.

And why not? That is what I want. But is it feasible? Is there anyone who trades options for a living?

Answer: YES.

There are many people who exchange life options. But most traders do not just hang on to options or stocks only. The ones I know trade all things - options, stocks, bonds, commodities, and even forex from time to time.

CAN YOU MAKE LIVING SELLING OPTIONS?

Yes again. If you do not extract anything else from my emails, I hope you will find that earning 10% on a commercial sale like an iron condor or a butterfly is not that difficult. We do it monthly. The trick is to avoid losses and manage your positions because not all trades win.

Many people make a living or supplement their retirement income with trading options. And the numbers continue to improve - just look at the trend of the volume of options. More and more options are exchanged each year. Volume figures are breaking records every year.

And if others can, you too. You do not need a rocket scientist or a genius. I know very stupid people who make good trading options. And thanks to technology upgrades, anyone at home has access to all the trading tools and data they need - almost all of them are available for free from your broker. Option trading fees are also lower than ever. So, consider trading options to make a living.

SO HOW MUCH CAN YOU EARN?

Most hedge fund directors would sell their first child with returns of 20% per year. Warren Buffet averages 22% a year and has been the richest man in the world for many years.

Before, I was aiming for 10% per month; now, I want 5% more per month. But even if we want less, say that 3% is still 36% per year. Try this at the bank.

HOW MUCH MONEY DO I NEED TO BEGIN TRADING OPTIONS FOR A LIVING?

It all depends on your lifestyle. If you reside in Texas, a 3,000 square foot home can cost $ 250,000 in a nice neighborhood. The same house would cost $ 750,000 in California. Do you need to ride a Porsche or Honda Accord that's right for you? Do you have 5 children to send to college?

The amount required depends on your expenses.

But to provide an answer to the question, let's say you want to make $ 100,000 a year. Cool.

If you want to earn $ 100,000 before taxes and commissions and get an annual return of 36%, you will need $ 277,777 in mutual funds. Now, I do not always use 100% of the money on my account. I leave about 20 to 30% in reserve. So, say you leave 20% in reserve too.

If you only redeem 80% of your account, you will need $ 347,500 in your account to earn $ 100,000 with a 36% return on risk money. Let's round that up to $ 350,000.

That's it? No, at least I do not think so. I think you should also have a decent amount of money for savings and other investments. For example, I have money from real estate and dividends, as well as some companies in which I have investments. So, if something bad happens to my trade or markets, I still have enough revenue to survive.

BUT WHAT IF YOU CAN TAKE RISK?

Ok, so you want to play and go bankrupt. I would always try to keep a 20% reserve on my account to overcome the losses and use it for adjustments and any good trading opportunities that may arise.

But if you take risks, get a portfolio margin. The margin of the portfolio is for traders who know what they are doing and allow you to trade in larger sizes with little money. So, with $ 100,000, you can trade up to $ 600,000 in options. WOW

This allows you to make money faster because you have more leverage, but you can also lose much faster - so be very careful. Greediness can make you do stupid things.

HOW LONG WILL IT TAKE ME TO LEARN TO TRADE OPTIONS?

It's a delicate question. It took me several years. I did not have any mentors or people to watch. There were also not as many websites, books, and videos available. I would say that if someone were serious and spent a few hours a day learning and negotiating, he could learn to change his life in a year. It will not be true for everyone, but I think it's a safe number to look for.

WHAT IF I DO NOT HAVE TIME TO LEARN HOW TO TRADE?

I don't like giving my money to other people to manage and then not knowing fully what they are doing with it. So, even if you are using a service like mine, which has self - trading, I think you should still know how negotiations work, how to use your broker's platform, and keep an eye on what's going on in your account. Some members told me that they only wanted to check their accounts once a year - that's stupid. It's your money. You worked hard there. And you have to work very hard to make sure that a) you do not lose it and b) keep growing.

SO, HOW POSSIBLE IS TRADING OPTIONS FOR A LIVING?

Yes, but it takes time, effort, and desire. Trading for a living is not always a hobby, or anything other than running your own business. It's not like in movies where they scream at their brokers over the phone to buy 1000 shares of this or that and earn a million dollars.

Take your time to learn how to trade. Remember, the markets will be here tomorrow. And with put options, each month is a new game; so if you miss this month, wait a few days.

You have two basic options when you trade stocks - you can create a long position to benefit when the price of a stock increases or create a short position to benefit when it falls. Along the way, you can get or pay dividends here and there, but that's pretty much the side of the bargain. The options allow you to benefit from stock movements up and down while offering some additional ways to capitalize on price changes.

By establishing a basic option position, it is possible to gain higher stock (buy) and lower (sell). In either case, your original investment is usually much lesser than a similar stock position. Also, to option positions, these securities can be combined to reduce costs further. This chapter provides ways to negotiate for less money and less risk.

LEVERAGING ASSETS TO REDUCE RISK

Generally, when you think about leveraging assets, you think about increasing your risk - at least on the equity side. The options allow you to leverage your assets while reducing your risky investment. It's a good combination. With options, the paid premium allows you to price a stock without placing 100% of its value. While there is no assurance that stocks will move in the desired direction, this is the case if you trade options or stocks. So why not do it cheaper?

DETERMINING YOUR TOTAL DOLLARS AT RISK

The options reduce the risk because less money is invested - that's the end result. Once a position has been created, anything can happen - stocks can go up quickly, fall like bricks, or sit down with minimal movement while the rest of the market is active. You do not know. Nobody knows what will happen next.

Any action can fall to zero; therefore, any long action or long position you hold may also be reset. Therefore, your initial investment is your maximum potential loss. In fact, I take it back - if you buy a stock using the margin, you could lose twice your initial investment.

The risk of a long equity position is considered limited but high. Indeed, an action can not fall below zero. Unfortunately, there is a probability of loss between zero and the price of some stocks.

However, there are many possibilities between a total loss and no loss. The main argument here is that when you invest with less money, in the beginning, you usually have less to lose. It is rare to have such a distinct advantage without any inconvenience. The distinct disadvantage of the options is that you can not wait for the change you expect from your investment because there is a time constraint.

Calling risk out when bullish

When you're optimistic about an action, you can:

- Create a long inventory position
- Create a long call position

If the stock goes up, you can take advantage of one of these positions - the extent of the benefit depends on the actual change. Your risk is reduced when you buy a call because it has reduced your total investment.

Two main things to note on the risk graph are:

- The significant difference in losses
- Profits increase faster with stock position

Because there are a number of trade - out in this business, I am going to take the slow accumulation of earnings with a lower total risk. It is certainly possible that the stock remains inactive for months, which makes me leave the position to begin a serious upward movement. Again, it's a business - off I'm ready to take.

A risk chart provides a very effective way to understand the risks, rewards, and trade-offs associated with a specific strategy.

By monitoring the values of the options, you will find that if the action moves slightly over time, the option can acquire and lose value as follows:

- Decreases or increases or as stock price rises or falls
- Increases or decreases as the implied volatility of the option increases or decreases.
- Decrease overtime

Price alone does not determine the price of an option. Implied contract volatility (IV) also plays a significant role in its value, with higher IVs resulting in higher contract values. The deterioration of time plays a minor role daily, but the cumulative effect may undermine the value of the option.

Establish long-term positions when implied volatility (IV) is relatively low to increase profitability and minimize losses due to IV reductions. Keep in mind that a relatively weak IR environment does not guarantee that the IR will increase during the lifetime of the option.

Making use of LEAPS for long-term option positions

This is a Long-term Equity Anticipation Security. It's not a new type of trading instrument; it's just a time-consuming option - more than six months to two years. All option stocks do not have LEAPS available, but for those who make the month due, it's almost always January. You will notice different root symbols for these options.

LEAPS goes something like this:

> • LEAPS contracts are made in May, June, or July; it depends on the option cycle.
> • The new contracts come due in January about 21 /2 years from the date of creation so that in August 2008, there are options available to 2 January 2010 and January 2011. 2011 is newly created jumps.
> • When new LEAPS are released, the closest January LEAPS (due in 2009) becomes a regular option, as Options Clearing Corporation (OCC) revises the symbol to include the root of the regular option.

The root symbol of a LEAPS contract is different from the root symbol of a specific stock to differentiate it from other January options that expire in different years. This approach to name LEAPS could become obsolete when the new option symbol program came into effect in 2008.

The abbreviation for a LEAPS contract comes from the security of anticipating long-term stocks. These contracts are simply options with a lot of time until maturity.

The more time you have for an option to expire, the more money you pay. Therefore, you should assume to pay more for LEAPS contracts. Your risk maximizes with this increased cost, but the extra time gives you a greater chance of maintaining a contract that is at stake (ITM) upon expiration. LEAPS are:

  • Available for some stocks and indices that have regular options.
  • An investment alternative was offering up to 21/2 years to benefit from your contractual rights.

In addition to giving more time to investment strategies, LEAPS offer extensive asset protection guarantees. The combination of LEAPS with a long stock significantly reduces the cost per day of protection. You must balance the reduced cost with the desired level of protection because, ideally, the inventory will increase over time as you hold it. If this occurs, the sales value decreases during this period, while the strike price remains the same.

More volatile stocks generally have a higher number of exercise prices available each month, as shares are more likely to reach a strike price further away.

Put limits on a bear in motion

When you are out of stock, you can:

- Create a short stock position
- Create a long sell position

If stocks fall, you can take advantage of any of these positions. Rewards are reduced because a stock can only go to zero. Similarly, the rewards are potentially great if the stock becomes worthless.

Two main things to note on the risk graph are:

- The significant difference in losses
- The less than a significant difference in earnings

TRUSTING MARKET TIMING

After trading for an indefinite period, you realize that it is very difficult to identify the future direction of security, let alone where it is going and when. But selecting an appropriate term for an option is clearly an important part of trading these securities. This means that you need:

- Recognize the role that ratings play in stock and option trading
- Be ready to be "wrong" and limit your losses.
- Pay the right price for realistic moves.

Basic option trading requires that you correctly predict the direction in which the underlying will move, the magnitude of the movement, and the maximum time it takes for the movement to take place. All of these things are also needed for stock trading - the difference is that you can keep a long position on stocks for months while trading. Managing a position in this way does not necessarily mean that you are trading successfully.

There are times when an action leaves a limited range, side channel, to return to the channel. If you have created a directional position based on the break, you must leave the position (action or option) if the action returns to the channel because the conditions that justified the trade no longer exist.

Predicting the right direction

To capitalize on a stock position or a single option, you must correctly identify the direction of the underlying stock movement.

Predicting the right direction is a challenge that you face, regardless of the security you choose, so it seems adequate to favor one that uses less of your capital for at least a portion of your transactions. Only you know the answer to that.

Here are some general rules to increase your chances of success:

- Trading with the trend using technical tools,
- Or (for competent opposites) negotiate against the trend when the moment is weakening, and its indicators point to a pending curve,
- Negotiating undervalued stocks that garner positive attention by using fundamental tools,
- In all trades, limit your losses with unbiased exit strategies.

Predict the extent of the move

The risk of time is the main disadvantage of trading options, but there is another risk that requires discussion. You may be right about the direction and timing of a stock move, and yet you have too small a range to make your option position profitable. This happens to all option operators.

How can you minimize these deficits? For the most part, it is useful to have some tools - technical or fundamental - that provide estimated price projections.

Your overall business profitability can be improved by focusing on more likely transactions (higher deltas indicating that the movement is more likely to occur) rather than less likely home run transactions. Let the gains accumulate over time, and you will probably have the chance to get a home run or two along the way.

Consider taking some of the profits from your table on a portion of your total position when the game you have planned is partially completed.

Options pricing models also help identify the most likely transactions by providing:

- Expected implied price evolution of the option (implied volatility)
- An estimate of the probability that the option will be ITM at maturity.

By using these option components in your trading analysis, you can determine whether the price of the option is relatively high or inexpensive by taking into account stock history, past option prices, and market conditions. This is shown later in an example.

Predicting the right moment

Time limits for an option give young traders their first rule-based system when risk is properly managed. It means both:

- Negotiation is a reasonable part of the account
- The position is closed before accelerating the decline

A long option position has a clear and integrated output rule. Ideally, this is not the only direction you use to get out of a position.

There is no one size for all maturity selection criteria, as they may vary depending on the strategy and your trading style. The most direct time horizon for options trading is associated with press releases or reports that may result in strong movements on a specific date. This includes:

- Economic or industrial reports, such as unemployment figures or semiconductor orders
- News Releases

Some technical tools also give estimated time projections, including price models or cycles. First, identify your time horizons and check the option strings.

COMBINING OPTIONS TO REDUCE RISK

A put was combined with long stocks to protect it, limiting the risk of the position. This was also accomplished when a call was added to a short stock position. In both cases, the cost of the position has increased.

The equilibrium level of a stock is simply the price of entry. Since option premiums cost you more than the contractual rights of the exercise price, an equilibrium value must be calculated using the strike price and the option price.

When you create positions that focus on specific market opportunities, you can combine the following:

- Stock options
- Set of different call options
- Different mounting options
- Call and collect

Adding long or buy options was the only combined positions discussed so far, but short options can also be used to minimize the risk:

- Further reduction of net position cost and / or
- By increasing the potential directions, the underlying can trade while making profits.

When a short option is correctly combined with a long option or the underlying stock of the same kind, it is said to be hedged. Indeed, your risks (obligations) under the short contract can be satisfied by using the shares or exercising your rights under the long contract. Without this protection, the short contract is called naked. It looks good for your exhibition.

Simple option trading allows you to receive a credit when opening a position - this credit is equal to the option premium. If all goes well, the option will expire without money (OTM), and you can keep the credit. Different newsletters encourage naked option strategies, and this may look like a great way to generate monthly revenue, but the seller needs to be aware of it.

Getting a naked call is the riskiest position you can create, and I strongly advise against this type of trading. Instead of creating a limited risk, an unlimited reward compatible with good risk management, a simple call is an unlimited risk, a limited reward position.

Unfortunately, what usually happens with these strategies is that months of small credits are eliminated with losses of one or two operations only against you. I am not opposed to the creation of a credit exchange; I just do not like to expose myself completely from the risk point of view.

The risk can be limited by combining credit or debit options using hedged option positions. This section presents limited risk allocation operations and combined limited rewards positions.

SPREADING THE RISK WITH A DEBIT TRADE

A vertical gap is a position that combines two options:

• A long option and a short option of the same type (buy or sell)

- Have the same month of maturity and different exercise prices.

This is called "vertical" because that's how exercise prices line up when you look at a chain of options. You can create a vertical gap for an initial debit or initial credit. In each case, the position presents a limited risk and reward.

Each option position in a vertical gap is called the leg.

The type of vertical spread you select depends on the outlook of your market. You Vary risks and benefits altering the strike prices used to establish the position too. You can create two kinds of vertical spreads for one debit, one using calls and the other using put options. They are referenced by inventory prospects and include:

Bullish Spread: You create a **bullish** spread by buying a call and simultaneously selling another call that expires in the same month. The short call has a greater exercise price. Short-term purchases eventually reduce the price of long-term purchases, so this spread trading is less risky than purchasing a purchase on its own.

Bear put spread: you make a bear put spread by buying a put and simultaneously selling another put expiring the same month. The put has a lower exercise price. The price of this lower strike being cheaper, you pay a net debit for trading. Short selling while reducing the long-selling price, so this spread trade is less risky than buying long sell options alone.

Exposing yourself is a very risky position, even if you are willing to buy the shares at the exercise price of the short sale. The sale of short selling generally occurs when the inventory is down or bad news is published. The acquisition of stock on the market or that the assignment in a time like this - it goes against reasonable risk management principles.

Risk Assessment and Reward for a Call Flow Spread

Your maximum risk for the upward spread is the initial debt you paid to create it, similar to a basic long position. Because the position combines a short call to reduce the cost of the long call, it also reduces the risk of the position. Because you get nothing for nothing on Wall Street, reducing your risk in this way has a price in terms of reduced rewards.

If ABC trades at $ 37.65 and you're up, you can create a higher spread by doing the following transaction:

- Buy on January 1st, call 35 @ $ 4.20 and
- Sell January 1, 40 Call $ 1.50

The buyer's long-term debt is $ 270 ([$ 4.20 - 1.50] × 100). This is also the maximum risk that occurs when

ABC closes at $ 35 or less upon expiration. At this price, both calls will be useless.

Unlike a basic long call, your all-out reward is limited by an increasing call spread because the short bond prevents you from getting unlimited rewards. Your maximum reward is the gain you get from year-end transfer transactions less than the initial debit paid for the $ 230 [($ 40 - 35) × 100 - 270.00] position. The maximum reward occurs when ABC is trading at $ 40 or more at maturity.

Your actual gain or loss can be between maximum risk and maximum reward if the ABC closes between 35 and 40. The calculation of the difference in profitability is similar to a long purchase. Using the Long Call Exercise Price, you add the difference between the two option prices (the initial charge without the multiplier) to determine your equilibrium level. In this example, the breakeven point is $ 37.70 (35 + 2.70).

Given that a vertical throughput differential is a net long position, its value will experience the same accelerated deterioration of time in the 30 days to maturity as a long default option position. Integrate a spread exit method before this period if the position may lose value in this way.

The risk map identifies the following important areas:

- Maximum risk $ 270 displayed by a lower horizontal line
- Maximum reward of $ 230 displayed by the top horizontal line
- A stock price of $ 37.70 displayed by a dark vertical line.
- A profit loss range, represented by a diagonal line ranging from the lowest strike price to the highest strike price.

Risk, reward, and balance calculations for vertical spreads are made assuming that you have been assigned your short bond and exercise your long rights.

Risk assessment and reward for a placed debit spread

Your maximum risk for the term spread is the initial debt you paid to create it, similar to a long base selling position. Because the position combines a short sale to reduce the cost of selling in the long run , it also minimizes the risk for the position.

If XYZ trades at $ 50.85 and you have lost stock, you can create a downward selling spread by doing the following:

- Buy on January 1st 50 put @ $ 2.75 and
- Sell on January 1st, $ 45 to $ 1.30

Net debt is also the maximum risk. The risk, reward, and profitability calculations are similar to those of the upward spread:

- Debt = maximum risk = (2.75 - 1.30) × 100 = $ 145.00
- Break-even = $ 50 - ($2.75 - $1.30) = $50 - $1.45 = $ 48.55

- Maximum Reward = [($ 50 - 45) × 100] - $ 145.00 = $ 355.00

The maximum reward occurs when XYZ is redeemed at $ 45 or less upon expiration.

The risk map identifies the following important areas:

- The maximum risk of $ 145 displayed by a bottom horizontal line
- Maximum reward of $ 355 displayed by the top horizontal line
- Price 48.55 $ breakage displayed ed on a dark vertical line
- A range of a loss of profit, displayed by a diagonal line ranging from the highest strike price to the lowest strike price.

Consider entering a vertical debit when there are at least 60 days left to expire to allow the position to become profitable.

Never leave the long leg of the vertical spread without also leaving the shortest side of the spread -

otherwise, you significantly change your risk profile. This applies even when it seems that the short leg will expire worthlessly.

Summarizing your debit risks and rewards

In the two vertical debit spreads, your risks and benefits are limited. Each spread is less risky than the corresponding long base position because you reduce the initial debt of the short option price. Risk reduction comes in the form of greatly reduced rewards for you because of the short position of the option also limits your profits.

A transaction risk graph provides specific risks, rewards, and tradeoffs associated with a specific transaction.

When ordering a new vertical flow differential, consider using a lower limit value than the cited price for the combined position to minimize the impact of slippage. You probably will not be able to trade at mid-spread, but you can probably get the order filled if you reduce the amount of debt a little bit.

HOW TO SPREAD THE RISK WITH A CREDIT TRADE

Debit spreads are not the only kind of spread trading that you can create using calls or put options. You can switch the purchased exercise price, and the one sold on the debit spreads to create a credit spread. Once again, the spread requires you to buy one option and sell another of the same type, expiring in the same month. You can build two different vertical credit spreads:

Bear call spread: You create a call distribution by purchasing a call and simultaneously selling another call that expires in the same month. The short call has a lower exercise price. Because the price of a lower strike call is higher, you get credit for trading. The long call ends up surpassing the short call, so this spread trade presents a much lower risk than a naked call option.

Bull put spread: You create a bearish spread by buying a put and simultaneously selling another put that expires the same month. The put has a higher exercise price. Because the price of a higher strike is higher, you get credit for trading. Long sales eventually cover short sales, so this spread trading is significantly lower risk than a short sale.

Risk Assessment and Reward for a Call Credit Spread

Your maximum risk for the bearish spread is limited to the difference between the strike prices of the options minus the credit you received when creating the transaction. The position uses long calls to limit the risk of short calls, which in itself is unlimited. Instead of placing an XYZ put spread for a debit, you can create a call spread call XYZ bear for a credit.

You create the bearish spread by buying the highest and cheapest call and selling the most expensive and lowest call:

- Buy on January 1st, 55 calls at $ 0.95 and
- Sell January 1st 50 Call @ $ 3.20

For credit spreads, net credit is also the maximum reward. The reward, risk, and break-even calculations for a bearish spread call are as follows:

- Credit = Maximum Reward = (3.20 - 0.95) × 100 = $ 225.00
- Break-even = $ 50 + ($ 3.20 - 0.95) = 50 + 2.25 = $ 52.25
- Maximum risk = [($ 55 - $ 50) × 100] - $ 225.00 = $ 275.00

A short purchase gap reduces risk by limiting short-lived losses. Reducing your risk means that your rewards are reduced. Your maximum reward is the initial spread credit. This occurs if XYZ closes below the exercise price of the short purchase at maturity, causing both worthless options to expire.

The risk map identifies the following important areas:

- The maximum risk of $ 275 displayed by the bottom horizontal line
- Maximum reward of $ 225 displayed by the top horizontal line
- A stock price of $ 52.25 displayed by a dark vertical line.
- A profit loss range, represented by a diagonal line ranging from the lowest strike price to the highest strike price.

If the original stock is close to the strike price on the last trading day prior to maturity, you may be given the short option on the weekend, but you may not have the option opportunity to exercise your contractual rights. long Close a vertical credit spread for debit on the last trading day before maturity if the underlying price is close to the short strike price.

Risk assessment and reward for a put credit spread

Your maximum risk for the Batch Spread is limited to the difference between the exercise prices of the options minus the credit you received when creating the transaction. The position uses the long sale method to significantly reduce the risk of short selling, which is high. Instead of placing a high ABC purchase gap for a debit, you can create a high ABC sales gap for credit.

You create a bullish spread by buying the lowest exercise put and selling the highest put:

- Buy on January 1st, 35 sales at $ 1.70 and
- Sell Jan. 1, 40 put @ $ 4.10

For credit spreads, net credit is also the maximum reward. The reward, risk, and break-even calculations for a stock gap are as follows:

- Credit = Maximum Reward = ($ 4.10 - 1.70) × 100 = $ 240.00
- Maximum risk = [($ 40 - 35) × 100] - 240.00 = $ 260.00
- Balance = $ 40 - ($ 4.10 - 1.70) = 40 - 2.40 = $ 37.60

A bull spread position reduces the risk by limiting the short put losses. Reducing your risk means that your rewards are reduced. Your maximum reward is the initial spread credit. This occurs if ABC closes above the strike price of the short sale at maturity, resulting in the expiry of the two options with no value.

Always watch the trading conditions after the close of trading on the last trading day before expiration. You never want to allow a limited-risk position to turn into a high risk or unlimited position because you can not manage the trade until the end.

Summarizing your credit risks and rewards

The risk chart for a vertical credit spread is similar to the vertical debit spread with limited risk and reward. It dramatically improves the short-term risk graph or short sale, which limits the risks are unlimited or limited, but high. This is done by creating a position that covers the short option instead of leaving it naked.

Although you can perform a spread operation at a price that is more favorable than the present market price, always remember that if your risk settings indicate that you need to leave a position, simply move out of the position. This can almost always be achieved by placing a negotiable term order.

When overall averages rise sharply, most equities and sectors do the same, and when they fall sharply, most stocks and sectors follow. The sectors do not move exactly in conjunction with the indices. Economic conditions often favor a group over a period of time, and as conditions change, so do sectors that show strength or weakness. Focusing on strong or weak areas allows you to apply the best strategies to the conditions. First, of course, you must know how to find them. Technical analysis provides tools to analyze sectors, including those to identify strengths and weaknesses. In this chapter, I present the fundamentals of technical analysis you need to achieve your sector trading strategies.

GETTING TECHNICAL WITH CHARTS

Chart analysis is an aspect of technical analysis that uses price and volume data to provide an overview of trends for market valuation purposes. There are a variety of graph types and data views, providing an extremely broad list of analysis tools. By focusing here on some industry-oriented and option-trading tools and techniques, novice traders in chart analysis should accelerate quickly, while those familiar with this will receive a review.

Basics of charts

The charts use price data to provide an overview of the trading activity over a period of time. A shortlist of common chart types includes the following:

Line chart: uses the price as a function of time. A single price data point for each period is connected using a line. It usually uses a close value, which is generally considered the most important value for the period (day, week, etc.). Line graphs provide excellent general information on   price movements and trends, filtering the noise of smaller movements during the period. period.

The disadvantages of line graphs are that they do not provide information on the strength of trading during the day or whether deviations have occurred from one period to another. A spread is created when trading a period is completely higher or lower than trading in the previous period. This happens when important news affecting the company comes out when the markets are closed. Does not it seem like a good piece of information to have when you negotiate?

Open-High-low-closed   bar   graph (OHLC): Uses the price as a function of time. The trading range for the period (from bottom to top) is displayed as a vertical line, with opening costs showed as a horizontal tab on the left side of the range bar, and closing prices in the form of a vertical line. horizontal tab on the right-hand side of the beach bar. break. A total of four price levels is used to build each bar.

OHLC charts provide information on the strength of the trading period and price differences. Using a daily chart as a reference point, a relatively long vertical bar informs you that the price range was wide enough for the day.

Another method to look at it is to say that stocks were volatile that day - good information for option traders. It also suggests a stock strength when stocks close near the high of the day and weakness when stocks close near the low of the day.

Candlestick chart: uses the price as a function of time. Similar to an OHLC chart with the open to the closed price range of the period highlighted by a thick bar. Unique patterns in this chart can improve daily analysis.

The candlestick charts have distinct interpretations of motifs that describe the battle between bulls and bears. It is better to apply them to a daily chart. Candlesticks also display price ranges and gaps.

See the graphs using both:

> • Long-term linear graphs observing price trends
> • OHLC chart or candlestick to better understand price action over the period,

including the strength and volatility of a
security

A wide variety of technical graphics packages are available as standalone software programs or web applications. The prices range from free to thousands of dollars, depending on the features of the package. When using technical analysis for the first time, consider starting with a free web package, identifying your specific needs, and developing from there.

REGULATING YOUR TIME HORIZON FOR THE GREATEST VIEW

Before you focus on a specific range of the chart, think about your investment or trading horizon. What you want to see when valuing your 401 (k) investment is different from your focus on active trading.

Technical analysis puts a different emphasis on deadlines. Long-term trends are considered stronger than those in the short term. To get the greatest view of trends, it's extremely useful to change the time range used for your charts. The typical chart pattern is a daily chart, but others also exist.

When performing a market analysis to find strong sectors, an ideal progression includes evaluating the following:

- Key Long-Term Trends Using Monthly Charts and Sector Charts
- Intermediate, major, and minor trends using weekly charts covering broad indices and industry sectors
- Small, short-term trends using daily pie charts

By first recognizing major and intermediate trends, you are less likely to be involved in the emotion associated with short-term movements.

A horizontal support line can be traced after lower prices to double the price level. The line is confirmed when the third ring of this price level is successfully maintained, and the purchase request returns to the title that submits the price.

VISUALIZING SUPPLY AND DEMAND

Charts can be seen as a display of supply and demand:

- Demand for purchase drives up prices
- Supply creates sales pressure that drives down prices
- The volume shows the magnitude of the supply or demand

Markets do not move up and down - the battle between bulls (demand) and bears (supply) causes different types of price movements.

A horizontal resistance line can be drawn when the price increases to reach the price level twice. The line is confirmed when the third ring of this price level is successfully maintained, and the sale of supplies returns to safety, which lowers the price.

Support and resistance areas

Support and price resistance are breaking the current trend:

  • Support represents a transition from supply-induced price declines to price increases when renewed demand comes into play at this price level.
  • Resistance represents a transition from rising prices, driven by strong demand, to lower prices when selling pressure reaches that price.

When negotiating, note that these transitions align over time, sometimes creating lateral trading channels as the price moves between the two. The more the price serves as support or resistance, the more it is considered strong.

The use of support and resistance to identify entry and exit points is a basic trading system. Also, consider using them in the price projections to identify stop losses and outflows as well as to calculate risk-reward rates.

Previously supported price zones tend to serve as areas of resistance in the future and vice versa.

Trend Analysis

I use the concept of trend a lot before reaching this formal definition. This is because I am sure you have an idea of what is an upward and downward trend for any asset. Painfully, if you held this asset in the latest trend. More formally, the trend identifies the direction of prices:

Upward Trend: the price go up and down so that a line on the rise can be traced in indentations that show higher lows. Higher highs are also characteristic of upward trends.

Downward trend: Prices fall and fall in such a way that a line of decline can be traced above the top of the retracement peaks, which have lower peaks. Low troughs are also characteristic of downward trends.

Create a trend line by connecting two lower (uptrend) or two lower (downtrend). When the price successfully tests the line for the third time, the trend is assured. Making use of these lines as entry and exit points is an effective application of the tool, similar to support and resistance levels.

Consider drawing two trend lines using a long-term chart , such as a monthly chart, to highlight a zone of resistance against a single subjective trend line. One can use close data while the other uses market lows. Follow the action of the market near everyone.

Moving Averages

Moving averages are lines constructed on a graph using an average closing price over a given number of days. These lines are considered late indicators because historical data follow price action. The two major kinds of moving averages are:

- Simple moving averages (SMA) using a basic average
- Exponential Moving Averages (EMAs) that integrate all available pricing data, adding weight to the latest data

Simple moving averages also weigh all closings over the selected period, while exponential moving averages are calculated so that the most recent data has more weight on the line.

SMAs and EMAs can be created using a variety of parameters and ranges of graphics. As a result, you can display a five-day SMA on a daily chart or a ten-week EMA on a weekly chart. Moving average lines are considered as unbiased trend indicators because the lines are derived from objective calculations.

The three most common parameters for any moving average are:

- 20-day moving average indicating short-term trends

- 50-day moving average indicating medium-term trends
- 200-day moving average showing long-term trends

You may have heard the financial media report that the price is close to the 200-day moving average. Indeed, a break in this line is considered significant and can confirm a reversal of the trend.

Exponential Moving Averages (EMA) incorporates all available price data for the underlying security, with newer data having a better weight on the EMA value for the period. Because of this, they are more sensitive to price changes.

IDENTIFYING RELATIVELY STRONG SECTORS

Bullish or bearish movements in the market generally lead to gains for most sectors and bonds. However, during more moderate trends, some sectors and stocks outperform the market, while others underperform. A sector or security may also move in the opposite direction during these periods. Your objective as a trader is to find relatively strong and weak groups so that you can apply lucrative strategies to the industry.

Relative ratios

You create a relative proportion line by dividing one title into another. This allows you to objectively show the performance of one security against another because the line increases when the main security exceeds the second and decreases in case of underperformance. Adding an overlay graph to a relative relationship allows you to display both titles in a graph. Ball ladders generally provide a better view of the movements of others.

Trend lines plotted on a log chart appear differently when you move to an arithmetic scale.

Shorter moving averages (i.e., a low setting) are considered faster and closer to price. You can distinguish these lines in a graph because they are a little jagged.

By including relative indices in a graph, you have a clearer view of the performance of two titles. When it seems that both indices have been moved in a similar way until very recently. But a look at the line of relative proportion tells another story. For much of the three year period, SPY outperformed the XLF, significantly from June to October 2007.

Relative report lines are also called relative force comparisons.

In a month of deterioration of the relative reason line, the XLF fell below the 200-day EMA and shortly after the 50-day EMA. Although unlabeled , the shorter EMA is identified by observing the one closest to the price. When the downward trend conditions are optimal, prices and MAs are aligned with the lowest price data that appears on the graph, followed by the shorter EMA then the higher EMA - just like this graph shows.

Some traders use moving average crosses as signals of the trading system. This approach has its place in the negotiations, but note, where the price was at the moment the cross occurred - almost at its lowest point. Keep in mind that moving averages delay price data. I like to use crosses to identify a change in inventory conditions and as a strategy filter. Once this crossing is done, I am in favor of downside strategies.

Before moving away from this particular graph, note that trend lines can be applied to relative proportions. The same rules apply:

- Draw upward trends using troughs
- Draw downward trends using trend highlights

In addition, the previous support areas can become robust and vice versa.

When you use overlay features in a chart, the indicators added to the chart are based on the primary security.

When using relative proportions, it is good to identify a group of indices or related sectors to monitor. Cash flow from one market or one industry to another as economic conditions change. Portfolio allocations should favor more efficient and underperforming markets. This results in the reversal of a market leader in another market for varying amounts of time.

The broad range of ETFs that track different assets (for example, the dollar or oil) allows you to use an asset allocation plan in the markets using only one type of security. Add options to many ETFs, and you have reduced the risk of accessing commodity and currency markets.

The curves trend can be used in the power lines comparison report to identify better the changing areas and conditions of support and resistance. Similarly, broken support will often serve as resistance in the future.

By focusing on the sectors, selecting an optional Family Family ETF allows you to assess industry trends and relative performance quickly. For example, Select Sector S & P Depository Receipts (SPDR) includes ten ETFs based on the S & P 500 Index:

- SPY follows the entire S & P 500 index
- Nine ETFs track each of the nine main sectors that make up the index

Collectively, the nine ETFs in the industry make up the SPY ETF. By examining ten graphs, you can conduct a broad market and industry assessment that can serve as a basis for overall investment or negotiations in the industry. The search for a liquid ETF fund family and optional your first goal, you do so a follow-up confirming the liquidity of ETF options.

A relative proportion line only compares the performance of two titles - it does not indicate a trend for either title. A rising line may indicate that the headline has an upward trend at a faster pace than the second headline or that it is trending downward at a slower pace.

RATE OF CHANGE INDICATOR

Relative proportions provide a good visual approach to evaluating sectors. A change rate approach allows you to quantify and rank the performance of these sectors. The rate of change (OCR) of a title is the speed at which it moves - when calculating safety returns, you use a type of OCR. There is also an OCR indicator that can be drawn on charts for the analysis, trading, or scoring of securities.

To calculate a ten-day OCR, use the following formula:

- (Price of the day ÷ Prices 10 days ago) × 100

As an alternative approach to industrial trade, you can expand the list to include industry groups, investment styles (small or large value, value, or growth) or countries, among others. The main objective is to develop a group of ETFs with related inflows and outflows.

By using OCR trends, you really want to capture the cash flow from one market or industry to another. Remember to check different times, such as weekly or monthly OCR, and see how notes change each week. Relative strength trading approaches aim to build upside positions on relatively strong performance and bearish positions on relatively poor performance. This worked best when the periods used entail ranking that persists for more than a week or two, so you stay in a strong position.

During trading, the ROC is used with a simple moving average (SMA) as a commercial alert. The ROC crosses above your SMA are bullish, and the ROC crosses under your SMA are a bearish alert.

The term normalizes refers to the process of expressing data so that it is independent of the absolute value of the underlying. This allows a comparison with other titles.

USING SECTOR VOLATILITY TOOLS

Technical analysis displays volatility in a number of ways, including historical baselines and volatility (HV)   charts. The objective technical indicators available in many graphic sets and covered in this section are:

- Statistical volatility
- Average True Interval
- Bollinger Bands
- Bollinger %b

These tools offer different views of volatility and allow you to check the markets for securities that can prepare for a change. Although volatility may remain high or low for long periods, these measures may provide the following:

- A purchase alert in case of decline
- A sales alert with higher heels
- A tool to help identify the appropriate strategies
- Seasonal motion detection

The value used for the technical indicators is called the parameter. Commonly used parameters are called default values.

Volatility display with indicators

Statistical volatility and the real average range are two different views of price movements. See how they differ:

Statistical Volatility (SV): VS, another term for historical volatility that makes use of closing values to show an annualized standard deviation line that signifies the degree of the price movement of the security. As various periods of time can be used in a chart, SV reflects the period of the chart, not necessarily a daily calculation, as you see on option HV or SV charts.

Average True Range (ATR): ATR used a true range value (TR) to define the price movement and was developed by Welles Wilder. The TR incorporates extreme movements, such as spreads, to better reflect volatility. TR uses the previous and
the last closing and closing values to calculate three different ranges. The widest beach for all three is the TR for the period.

A rate of return calculation is a measure of the rate of change. It allows comparisons of securities at different prices, creating value regardless of price.

ATR is an exponential moving average that smooths TR. A big change in ATR incorporates price differences and provides traders with important information on price volatility that may be missed by other smoothed indicators. As ATR uses historical prices and a smoothing process, it is a lagging indicator and does not predict volatility. However, a strong upward movement of the ATR of a bond is often accompanied by an IV increase in its options.

When using brokers to identify low bandwidth inventory, check the chart to see what is happening with the stock. The price may have fallen due to an ongoing securities transaction such as a stock purchase and is less likely to change from this point on.

The nine sectors ETFs hit the lowest on the same day, with each ATR peaking in the next day. The SV profile of ETFs varied more, but most also peaked a few days before the bottom. When reviewing charts, note the following about XLI:

- The price has evolved over a very wide range, closing the day in style with a slight net gain.
- SV was moving away from a peak two days earlier
- ATR always went up
- The 14-day SMA ROC was flat, suggesting a possible end to decline.

Although XLI ranks fifth on the 14-day ROC, closing at its highest for the day was extremely optimistic, given the variety of trades that day. The situation deserved surveillance to confirm a reversal.

The price continued to climb, while the ATR appeared to decline, and SV conditions remained high. The ROC exceeded its 10-day ADM, which was a bullish signal. The only strategy discussed so far that adapts to these conditions (high volatility, high) is a long and short buying position.

By buying the close ETF at $ 38.55 and selling the September 39 exercise price at $ 0.80, you created a moderately reduced risk position. Instead of $ 3855 on the line, you reduced your exposure to $ 3775 or 2%. In fact, there are better strategies to take advantage of this situation - ones that allow you to limit your risk a lot more - but this is appropriate for now.

You can create a short-term covered call strategy in order to be excluded from the position. This is the case here, so you want the XLI to trade above 39 by the September due date. That's exactly what happened. At maturity, Friday XLI closed at 40.63, and you would have been affected. That means you bought the position for $ 3,775 and sold it for $ 3,900.

ANALYZING VOLATILITY WITH BOLLINGER BANDS

The Bollinger Bands provide another interesting insight into relative volatility levels. This technical tool makes use of a simple moving average (SMA) surrounded by upper and lower ranges, both derived from a standard deviation calculation. John Bollinger, the developer of the tool, uses the following parameters as default settings:

- SMA 20 periods

- The upper band (SMA + two standard deviations)
- The lower band (SMA - two standard deviations)

Bands expand and contract as price volatility contracts and spread.

Two additional Bollinger Band tools are:

Bandwidth (BW) for measuring the distance between the two bands using the calculation: BW = (BB higher - BB lower) Average moving average

Bollinger has shown that when BW is at its lowest level in six months, a tightening candidate is identified. It is a security that consolidates before a potentially strong leak, bigger or smaller. It is common for a false move to occur so that comprehensive strategies can provide a way to remedy this situation.

% b to know where the price is relative to PV, calculated using a variation of George Lane's stochastic indicator, with values ranging from:

- 0 to 100 when the price is equal or between ranges
- Less than 0 below the lower band
- Greater than 100 above the upper band (high)

Review the news when you come across a chart with a sharp rise or fall in prices, as well as a narrow bandwidth in the Bollinger Bands.

A value of 75 reflects the price in the bands and a quarter below the lower band in terms of total bandwidth. % b normalizes the price to the size of the bandwidth and allows you to compare apples with apples from different stocks for sorting purposes.

Different industries are experiencing bullish and bearish trends at different times. Although large ups and downs in major markets often move all securities in the same direction, the strength and duration of movements of these different securities may vary considerably. In general, the following applies:

Sectors and securities with very high values for% b are optimistic when confirmed by other technical tools.

Securities and sectors with values too low for% b are low when confirmed by other technical tools.

Bollinger noted that instead of prices being raised when they are close to a Bollinger Bands, the condition actually reflects the strength and a leak that can continue. Look for setbacks towards the moving average line to establish new positions in the direction of the trend after such a break.

PROJECTING PRICES FOR TRADING

There is no guarantee on the markets. Options with low levels of implied volatility may remain low, downside stocks may continue to decline, and options with a 75% chance of making money at maturity, depending on the model, may expire worthlessly. That's why risk management is your first job as a trader. Using resistance areas and support areas and trend lines is a simple way to manage your risks.

Price projections can include those that identify outputs for a loss or profit. Both are important. Sometimes we focus so much on risk management that we also forget not to forget to make a profit. By identifying areas higher and lower than the current price before establishing a position, you simplify the management of operations. Consider using objective strategies like price channels, retractions, and extensions to identify output levels. The following sections present the two sides of the coin: methods for projecting price movements (magnitude and time) as well as risk management tools. Exactly what options traders need.

SUPPORT AND RESISTANCE

Support and resistance provide subjective tools that identify:

- Actual output levels for loss
- Potential exit levels for profit

Although the support and resistance lines are subjective, they represent a reasonable approach to manage your risk because they identify a maximum loss. As your skills develop, the application of these tools and exit points will be improved.

The reason I use the "potential exit" on the profit side is that changing conditions can guarantee an anticipated exit from partial profits or allow you to increase revenue based on the change. Suppose you embrace a bullish position - if your indicators become bearish, you may receive an alert requesting a position exit earlier than expected. Similarly, you may have already received a portion of your profits when the title reaches its original projection price. If the chart stays bullish, you can review your price target for additional profits.

The extent of the exit only applies to the profit; the exit points for a loss must be fixed in the stone. You can move earlier, but you absolutely can not revise the output level in a way that increases losses. It is essential to identify a maximum loss price for the position and execute it if it is reached.

As the trend lines are traced by the analyst, a certain degree of bias can be introduced. Consider giving yourself some freedom when using these inbound and outbound pricing areas to help reduce the impact of bias.

Making use of a moving average crossover system, you decide to take a long position in the XLF (Financial ETF) the day after the 20-day EMA cross-over by the 50-day EMA. An output signal includes a

20-day EMA cross below the 50- day EMA. Because this output does not identify a specific output for a loss, you add a helpline below the present price to manage your risk.

In the previous uptrend, $ 36.58 support, but this zone was halted when the XLF went down a few months ago. Since then, the market has reversed, and the same level of $ 36.58 had served as resistance when the XLF began to rise. The ETF has recently surpassed this level, making it a reasonable area of support for future stop loss. Since the ETF trades around $ 37.10, it represents a 1.4% loss in risk parameters.

To display a 200-day moving average on a weekly chart, you must use a setting of 40 because there are five business days in a week.

Longer moving averages are considered slower and less sensitive to price changes. You can distinguish these lines in a graph because they are softer. The calculation of a moving average is called the smoothing process.

TRENDS

Trend lines are ascending and descending moving lines drawn through higher troughs (upward trend) or lower troughs (downward trend). These lines can also be used for price projection purposes. The actual price level used with these lines is estimated because the lines tend rather than horizontal.

Many technical analysis packages include a targeting tool that allows you to identify the price and date for different areas of the chart. Using the same XLF EMA cross entry technique, a trendline output can be identified with the crosshair tool.

Many trend tracking systems have more small losses and fewer large profitable transactions. These systems depend on the use of the system output rather than physical stop-loss output levels. To properly manage risk while letting the system function properly, it incorporates the percentage of loss outflows in its back-test to determine if the system is viable when a stop loss is included.

The options come with an expiration period, so the time it takes for a stock to reach a projected cost is as important as the projection itself.

There are many technical tools that generate input and output signals but not price projections. When identifying a maximum loss exit point, be sure to consider basic risk management techniques.

CHANNELS

Price channels include those designed using two different trend lines and those built using a regression line - here I show the last one to focus on objective tools. A regression channel:

- Uses a specific number of previous prices to create the chain
- Includes an intermediate regression line representing the expected value of future prices (without guarantee)
- Corrects the data period, then extends the channel lines forward in time.

A regression line is fixed, which means that it is constructed using data with a start and end date rather than adding and deleting data in the same way as a moving average. The price should reverse the average with these channels.

A regression line is also called a line of best fit. This is the line that represents the shortest distance between each data point and the line.

When building a regression channel, you make use of an existing trend that must remain intact. The price contained in the channel confirms the trend, and the outgoing price of the channel suggests that a change of trend could develop.

There are several ways to create a string. Here I focus on a basic approach to linear regression. After recognizing the trend period, the regression line is drawn, and the limit lines are created as follows:

- The upper limit uses the distance between the regression line and the highest point on the line.
- The lower limit uses the distance between the regression line and the lowest point on the line.

The very wide canals reflect volatile tendencies, while the narrow canals reflect quieter tendencies. Often the price will stay in the upper or lower channel for periods of time. If the price comes out of the channel and returns to it without going to the median regression line, a change of trend could develop.

Suppose you created the regression channel using a weekly OHLC bar graph for XLB. The data range for the channel is indicated above, and a long entry point in the trade is identified by the arrow.

As the trend progresses, you can identify an increasing exit point using the lower limits of the channel and the regression line. Your exit rules may include the following:

- Exit the position Monday after the price closed the lower channel line on the weekly chart (projected at 25.36).
- Make a profit if the price rises above the upper channel line then return to the channel.
- Make partial profits on the middle regression line if the price is not shifted to the upper channel line.

See the help links in the chart set for information on creating and applying metrics.

Using the crosshair tool allows you to identify realistic price projections that correspond to points in future time.

Try building regression channels on weekly and monthly charts, then switching to daily and weekly charts, respectively, to apply robust trends to the relatively shorter period.

Although very hard to see in the image, the reticule tool also identifies March 12 as the corresponding date for moving to the lower boundary line. In other words, assuming the price continues to behave as in the past.

You may think it's a very big assumption, but it's the one you make every time you get into a trendsetting position. This approach of a temporal projection is subjective but provides a good check of reality when considering the possible movements.

Trends are not considered predictive. They exist on the market, but they do not predict the price because they can continue or fail. The technical tools provide guidelines for risk management and profitability, not guarantees.

Retractions and price extensions

Rewind tools use existing trends to identify potential areas of support and price resistance. The trends and market conditions are largely associated with two primary human emotions: greed and fear. Technical analysis recognizes the impact of this crowd-based behavior and uses tools that attempt to quantify it when possible. One of these applications includes the use of Fibonacci rates for retraction purposes. These proportions are derived from a numerical series of the same name, originally defined by Leonardo Fibonacci.

Series Examples and proportions are found in nature and are used by many traders. How different market players take ã measures when certain n e levels before ç Fibonacci are met, you need to be aware of these levels. A basic understanding will probably help you evaluate the market action.

WD Gann was a successful product trader who also developed a number of widely used indexes and retraction and extension tools. Gann's ratios include, among others, 0.125, 0.25, 0.50, and 1.00.

Series and proportions of Fibonacci

The entire Fibonacci series is generated starting with 0 and 1 and adding the two previous integers in the series to get the next integer

Fibonacci rates are values obtained by dividing an integer in the series by previous or next integers specific to the series.

As prices do not increase up or down, contractions develop, which are counter-trend movements. A retracement includes:

- A retraction of prices during an uptrend
- A rise in prices during a period of decline

Fibonacci levels are often used to define withdrawal zones. Extensions use the same aspect ratio process to identify projections beyond the starting point of the base trend.

Fibonacci numbers can be used to configure indicators to make adjustments to the default value.

Time extensions

A second method uses Fibonacci numbers or proportions to identify future dates of possible turns. Projections are determined using

- A ratio based on the time needed to create the original trend.
- A count using progressing Fibonacci integers.

Another approach commonly applied to time objectives is the use of market cycles. Similar to the economic cycle, the stock market goes through ascending and descending cycles, which are measured from bottom to bottom. A low cycle can then be used to estimate the next low potential for the market. One of the best-known cycles of the stock market is the four-year cycle, with a recent trough in 2006. For the future, this means that another important minimum is expected to develop in 2010.

PROJECTIONS AND PROBABILITIES

By aligning different high probability factors, you create a situation where you place the odds in your favor for a specific strategy or operation. By managing your risk, you minimize losses and make larger gains . The process involves some science (supported by rules) and some of the art (supported by experience).

Possibility of weighing versus probability

Although basic tools can be subjective, a valid trend line makes it easier to identify intact trends and provides a sensible exit point when the line is broken. This interruption is a sure sign that the original reason for entry into the trade is no longer valid. However, you can still encounter problems when the time comes.

What happens if the trend line you drew was on a weekly chart, and during the week, the trend line was broken? Technically, you do not have a weekly close below the trend line, but that does not mean you should just continue to see the price deterioration. The technical methods rely on the confirmation of the indicators to help align the ratings.

Identifying an exit point before entering a position helps to reduce your excitement during trading.

During an uptrend, if the volume increases as the price fall towards the trend line, it will be a downward warning. A line break with increasing volume is another proof of bearishness. This action on a daily chart allows you to leave an established position using weekly data.

There is no assurance that the trend will remain intact.

Waiting for all the tools to become optimistic will generally not lead to negotiations. Or those who are marked will be created at the end of a movement. Try to evaluate the conditions and use their experience to put all the chances of your name. Although XLI has increased and trade has progressed, the same conditions on a different day may lead to continued downward movement. That's why risk management is essential.

React to the anticipation of a movement

Anything can happen on the markets next week or the trading day. . . even when the market closes. Trends can continue, reverse, or simply stop. The more time goes by, the more uncertain things become, so it's always good to remember that you just do not know what's going to happen tomorrow. The best you can do is to identify the rules of risk management and to maintain the odds in your favor. When conditions change, take the necessary steps and continue.

Practice disciplined trading through these strategies to gain the experience necessary to hone your skills in different market conditions:

Sector Analysis: When performing an analysis, use tools that provide objective information about current conditions for different time periods, including moving averages and Bollinger bands. This lets you stay in step with what is happening with what might happen next. Consider the general movement of the market and the evolution of the industry in relation to the market.

After assessing the current trend and volatility conditions, incorporate other tools that provide insight into the strength of these conditions and possible changes. Then develop your strategy accordingly.

Only accept new positions if you can effectively manage all your open businesses.

Commercial evaluation: When evaluating potential business use tools that provide reasonable projections to evaluate reward : risk rates. Consider only the position with the risk levels that is within your guidelines.

Operations Management: When managing a position, be sure to monitor the conditions - do not stray from an operation that requires your attention. Use order types that automatically perform a stop-loss exit when possible .

By adding option strategies to your investment and trading portfolios, you minimize trading stress. Trading is quite difficult, but when market conditions threaten your long-term holdings, distraction can be quite destructive. Stress reduction is very vital to better decision making in both aspects of your portfolio.

Options protect portfolios and trading positions. Because there are several strategies available, you must have an implementation plan. In this chapter, I discuss some protection strategies and some things to consider when you put them into practice.

The last part of the chapter discusses a unique risk that adjusted options represent for investors and traders. Adjusted options are contracts with a non-standard delivery package due to securities transactions that occurred during the term of the option. I discuss the options defined here as they may add risks even to the conservative and protective strategies included in this chapter.

PUTTING PROTECTION ON LONG STOCK

I usually focus on short-term options trading strategies in this book, but the options are also definitely geared to long-term holdings. Applying protection strategies to your existing reserves can turn anxious, sleepless nights into quiet nights during market crises. Since no one knows when these slowdowns will occur, integrating protection strategies as a regular consideration in your investment planning can mean the difference between reaching your financial goals in time or standing by for the next bull run to get there. arrive.

COMBINING PUTS WITH LONG STOCK

The purchase applied to existing equity investments provides insurance against large losses in the event of a major downturn. As with other forms of insurance, it's frustrating to write a check for something you may not need, but it's great to have it when the time comes. Two strategies that combine a long inventory with a long investment are:

- Married put (stock and sale bought together)
- Protection put (stock and product purchased separately)

The two positions are basically the same but are different in the pure- chases calendar. Each consists of a long purchase for every 100 shares held. It is not necessary to distinguish the terms. What is important for you is to understand why and how you protect your assets. I use the term protection post for the rest of this chapter.

129

A put gives you the right, but not the obligation, to sell the underlying shares at the exercise price of the contract until the business day preceding the expiration date of the option. Until now, you can also sell this right on the market.

Protection considerations

The phrase is sometimes used to describe the stock market and its tendency to all actions "all boats of rising tide raises" to raise together during a bullish run. Unfortunately, the opposite is also true. Whatever the merits of individual action, when a low market reaches, it does not take prisoners - to fall quality actions.

It is almost impossible to anticipate market fluctuations, so the best thing to do next is to protect the reserved shares in the long run. Suppose you bought ABC shares a few months ago for $ 34.00 and want to keep them for the long term. You can, at any time, set a selling price for this stock by buying a sale. It does not matter whether you intend to exercise some of your losses or simply offset them with option gains.

When considering two different equity investments with similar growth potential and prospects, check the available options. This can facilitate your investment decision if one allows you to buy protection while the other does not.

Instead of an all-or-nothing approach that includes selling ABC and attempting to buy back in the event of a market downturn, the position can be protected in the short or long term using the put. Before considering specific options, you must decide to continually protect a position or do it intermittently, depending on your market prospects.

Suppose you are looking for temporary protection for ABC (30 to 60 days). When reviewing option strings, you will need to evaluate the options 60 to 90 days before they expire. This gives you the flexibility to move away from the position before the decay of time speeds up 30 days before expiration. The next thing to consider is the level of protection you want to have. Table 10-1 provides partial sales chain data for ABC to assist in this decision.

Open interest implies the total number of open contracts for a specific option contract. Since option contracts are created on-demand, they reflect information about the trading activity of the day before.

One size does not fit all

Because you are concerned about the market action in September and October, it is reasonable to focus on the October and January options to cover the downside. You must then identify any losses that you wish to accept. You bought the title for $ 34, and you are currently trading at $ 37.50. Do you want ABC protection at the current price or the level you bought it? These are questions that you face every time you consider protecting a position.

The longer the time it takes to mature, the more uncertain the share price will be at maturity. An in-the-money (ITM) has more time to become an out-of-the-money (OTM) and vice versa. The price of options uses the movements after the inventory to assess the different probabilities for the future movement of the pre ç them. Use delta as an element to check the probability that the option will be ITM upon expiration, given its past movement.

Although protection is a relatively simple strategy, there are many ways in which protection can be provided. To help you in your analysis, identify your horizon of protection and the maximum loss you are looking for before viewing the option strings. This will help you make decisions.

Price of exercise of put options - Prime purchase = POS options (purchase value at the point of sale - purchase price) × 100 = Net income

Unless otherwise indicated, the multiplier of a stock option is 100. When trading with a combined position that includes 100 stocks, be sure to incorporate this value into the formulas.

From that moment, the actual option selected for the strategy is definitely a personal decision. You may prefer long-term protection and include April options in your valuation. You can only search for catastrophic coverage , in which case you can also add exercise prices below 35.00.

To close the example, warning 37.50 must be selected if you do not want to see a lucrative position turn into a loss during the exercise. If you are pessimistic in October, the ABC Jan 37.50 put option offers protection for the entire period.

There are many things to ponder when looking for protection for an existing inventory position, including:

- Term of protection (month due)
- Level of protection (strike price and the option price)

You can also consider the probability that an option will be ITM at maturity by referencing the delta. By using the options most likely to be ITM at expiration, you may find that you can get out of the protective position and use the product to help fund new protection.

You can still sell a hedging option before it expires if you believe the markets have calmed, and the intermediate outlook for your stock is back.

Since nobody knows what the next day will bring to the markets, an investor may decide to maintain a certain level of protection in-stock positions, regardless of the short or intermediate perspective. To minimize expenses, lower strikes can be considered as part of a plan that offers a cover catastrophic - a type of protective approach against collisions.

Accelerated decay of time

When negotiating options for this or other policies, you must consider the impact of time lag on the position of the option. Theta is the Greek option that identifies the daily loss of option value associated with the current price of the option.

Using an ABC Out 37.50 put option with 60 days to expire, you can get a theta by accessing an options calculator such as the one located on the ICO website (www.optionscentral.com).

The theta value of the option traded at $ 1.05 is - 0.0078. This means that if everything stays the same tomorrow, the option will lose 0.0078 in value. This may not be much, but it may increase.

In addition to the cumulative impact of weather deterioration, this rate accelerates as the expiry approaches, particularly during the last 30 days of an option's life.

The impact of weather deterioration accelerates the last 30 days of an option's life. This means that the extrinsic value will decrease more quickly with the value of the option - assuming all other circumstances remain the same.

To reduce the impact time decay within 30 days of expiration, long-term option trading strategies must incorporate an exit plan that resolves the problem. Generally, I leave an option 30 days before maturity to avoid accelerated losses of its extrinsic value.

If you think that $ 0.02 / day is manageable, consider what it means in terms of percentages. In ten days, 0.0216 represents 4.8% of the value of the contract.

The way you protect your positions is similar to any other investment decision - it depends on your personal preferences or risk tolerance. Find an approach that suits your style.

Weighing protection cost versus time

When you have a specific and reasonably short time horizon to protect a position, the month selection is quite simple. Once you look for long-term protection, the analysis requires a little more effort. Because you expect security to increase in the long run, ATM options must be OTM by maturity and can be very inefficient. You must weigh the cost of protection against the duration of the validity of the protection.

The investment process requires that you balance risk and reward. No risk, no reward, but that does not mean you have to risk everything. Consider protection positions as a way to limit your losses while letting your profits run.

Long-term protection

Suppose you have observed that XYZ shares have recorded steady annual gains of 8%, even over the years, with a 2% drop in the course of the year. How do you protect this position? A $ 2.15 GAB offering five months of protection was used in the ABC example. Since ABC was $ 37.50, the sales premium represents 5.7% of its value.

Balancing the cost of protection and returns is difficult and requires a game plan. Again, this is not a unique proposition for all proposals. If you regularly buy put options, you may sacrifice the returns stock and more. On the other hand, completely ignoring protection can cost a large part of your initial investment.

The simple solution to this issue is that you need to find the right balance for you. You can decide to use the intermittently put options when it emerges weak periods, but if you can synchronize the markets as well, probably not need protection. Think about it.

When buying products to protect your investments, be sure to balance the cost of protection against the net returns of the protection position.

By carefully evaluating the different options, rather than simply looking for the cheapest alternative, there is a greater chance that the option will be worth 30 days before expiration. As part of your plan, consider:

- The net exercise value and the level of protection provided
- The net impact on returns versus the cost of protection

- The statistical chance of the option being ITM at expiration (delta)

Being clear about your strategic goals from the start should definitely help you.

Calculation of costs per day

Finally, when selecting the protection elements:

- Be careful when buying seemingly cheap products that do not offer adequate protection and will likely expire worthlessly.

- Consider the cost of protection during the maintenance period of your actions.

Using ABC's strike price of 37.50, you can calculate the daily protection cost for both options. This is done by dividing the option premium by the number of days before expiration:

- ABC October 37.50 put @ \$ 1.05 = \$ 1.05 × 100 = \$ 105
- \$ 105 ÷ 60 days = \$ 1.75 per day
- ABC \$ 37.50 put @ \$ 2.15 = \$ 2.15 × 100 = \$ 215
- \$ 215 ÷ 150 days = \$ 1.43 per day

The selling price of ABC Jan 37.50 translates into a cost of approximately \$ 0.014/share for the option if held to maturity.

Try your best to manage your positions by responding to market conditions without reacting excessively. Nobody can completely control their emotions when the markets go up or down. Do what you can to manage them by completing your analysis when markets are closed whenever possible.

LIMITING THE RISK OF SHORT STOCK WITH CALLS

Long options offer a way to protect your investments for a specific period of time. Although you probably do not have short equity positions in your investment portfolio, you can periodically trade strategies that use short overnight equity positions. A long call can protect you against losses due to ascending nocturnal breaks.

Protecting a short position

Just as a long sell option protects a long stock position, along with buy, protects a short stock position. An appeal gives you the right, but not the obligation, to buy shares at a specific exercise price on the maturity date. You can exercise your purchase rights to close a short position if the shares increase rapidly.

Because a short stock position is generally maintained for less time, it is much easier to select protective purchase options. Generally, you can evaluate options as soon as possible until the expiration or next month. Shares with options will have two months available.

The option months closest to expiration are usually called *next- month options* and those that expire shortly thereafter are called *next-month options*.

In addition to paying less for the call, the selection of the strike price should be easier because the stock is less likely to move away from the entry price in the moderately short period the position is held. Try to use options that meet your criteria for maximum loss.

Continued reduction of the risk of short stock

If you are really want to reduce the risk of out of stock, why not consider setting up a long sales strategy to capitalize on your bearish vision for a specific stock? Suppose you do not have ABC shares, and you have low stocks. How does a long sell position compare to a short stock position? Assuming ABC is trading at $ 37.50.

Here's what you need to consider:

Cost of inventory: The initial cost for the short stock position is 50% of the current stock price because selling a margin required 150%. 100% is credited to the account for the sale of shares, and the remaining 50% is the money you need for the position.

The maximum risk of inventory: Because the inventory can theoretically increase without limit, the risk for a short seller is also considered unlimited. You can try to limit this risk by asking that the shares be bought back if they exceed a certain price, but overnight deviations inaction may cause this maximum level of risk to be exceeded.

Risk of maximum option: the maximum exposure for a long option position is the premium paid. In this case, it's $ 105.

Option Maximum Reward: If you have the right to sell one share for $ 37.50, and you are currently trading at $ 0, the intrinsic value of the option will be $ 37.50. Theoretically, you can buy shares on the market for $ 0, then exercise your right to sell them for $ 37.50. The $ 1.05 you have paid for this right must be subtracted from the gain of $ 37.50 per share of the stock transaction to determine the maximum reward for the position of the option.

Option Break-even Level: The break-even point of the option's position is the strike price option minus the option price, or $ 37.50 to 1.05 = the US $ 36.45.

The value of the places increases when a stock falls and represents a bearish position. Although they waste assets that are adversely affected by the deterioration of time, they have limited risk and limited but high reward potential.

Looking first at your risk, the short position limits the maximum risk to $ 105. This equates to an amount of $ 1.05 per share that can easily be overcome with a night inventory gap. From the point of view of the reward, you reduce the maximum gain by the cost of the sale ($ 105), but you have the potential to far exceed the small reward in stock by comparing the margin gains.

HEDGING YOUR BETS WITH OPTIONS

You can use the following options to hedge stock positions:

- A long position with a long stock position
- A long call with a short position

The option may be exercised to close the position of the shares, or optional gains can be used to offset the losses in the shares. The term *hedge* talks about a position used to offset losses on security resulting from adverse market movements.

Securing a position or portfolio with options is a form of hedging. But not all covers are created equal. . . some are more perfect than others. A *blanket perfect* is a position that includes a title that earns the same value as a second title. The gain outweighs the loss. As a result, a $ 1 decrease in ABC coincides with a $ 1 increase in XYZ.

The Greek options delta obtained using an option calculator provides the expected change in the value of the options given a $ 1 change in the underlying stock.

Protect a portfolio. . . partially

You partially protect a position when you have a security that gains value when the hedged position loses value. In general, when you combine two titles that tend to move in opposite directions, you find that it is not always an individual relationship. A gain of $ 1 on one share may be a loss of $ 0.75 on another security. Assuming that the relationship between the two continues, their combination offers a partially protected position.

Delta can be used to help create partially or completely covered positions.

Coverage of shares with stock options

The ABC 35.00 put has a delta of -0.186. Assuming you own 100 ABC shares and sell on October 35, the expected impact on your account with a $ 1 drop-in ABC is calculated as follows:

- (Underlying change) × (Delta) = Change of option (-1) × (-0.186) = +0.186

When the stock drops to $ 36.50, the option is expected to increase to about $ 0.54. The stock position lost 100 dollars, and the option position gained about $ 19. Since the entry into force on October 35, when the value of the shares has lost value, she has provided coverage for ABC. However, the gain on the option was less than the loss of shares, so it is only a partial hedge of the position.

The listed indexing options have characteristics different from those of listed stock options. For example, a hint is not a security for you, not something you can buy and sell. As a result, index options are settled in cash rather than when transferring a physical asset.

Cover a portfolio with index options

Since listed options are available for stocks and indices, portfolios can be hedged individually or with index options, assuming that the portfolio is well correlated with a specific index. Securing your portfolio may actually require an index option for a group of shares and individual stock options for others that are not well correlated with a particular index.

Correlation is used to describe the relationship between sets of data. Values range from -1 to +1, and once it's been applied to actions, you provide the following information:

- Equities whose returns move in the same direction of the same magnitude say they are positively correlated positively (+1)
- Equities with returns moving in the opposite direction of the same magnitude that would be perfectly correlated negatively (-1)
- Stocks whose returns do not change consistently in terms of direction and magnitude are considered uncorrelated (0)

For example, suppose you have a well-correlated $ 150,000 OEX portfolio trading at around 680. A quick partial hedge approach uses the value of the portfolio and the strike price of the index to estimate the hedge. OEX index options are obtainable for different months in five-point increments of the exercise price. When trading at 682, a purchase of 680 will have an intrinsic value of $ 2 because the value of the option is the same for index and equity options.

A common multiplier for an index is also 100, so the total option premium for the March 670 sale is $ 1,050 ($ 10.50 × 100). The basket of options is valued using the strike price and the multiplier, or $ 67,000 for sale on March 6 (670 × 100).

The option multiplier is the contract valued to determine the net premium of the option (market price of the × multiplier option) and the value to be delivered from the set of options (strike price of the option). ' option × multiplier).

Suppose you decide to protect your portfolio against market declines of more than 2%. You can estimate the hedge by starting at the current index level (682) and subtracting the decline you want to accept to get a starting point for the strike price selection as follows:

- 682 - (682 × 0.02) = 13.6
- 682 - 13.6 = 668.4

Exercise prices 665 and 670 can be taken into account. Using the 665 Put Option:

- Protection offered by 1 put: 1 × 665 × 100 = $ 66,500
- Protection offered by 2 Puts: 2 × 665 × 100 = $ 133,000
- Protected Portfolio: $ 133,000 ÷ $ 150,000 = 88.7%

If OEX falls below 665, your sales are gaining intrinsic value at a rate equal to the sales delta. As the OEX decreases, the peaks are closer to a 1: 1 movement with the index. The time remaining before expiry will also affect the actual coverage gains.

Cash options (ATMs) have deltas of approximately 0.50. Once an option is passed from ATM to in the money (ITM) or out of money (OTM), the delta changes value. The Greek option that gives an idea of the amount of delta change is gamma.

A set of stock options generally represents 100 shares of the underlying stock. When you use the strike price and the 100 multipliers to evaluate the options package, it is common to think that you pay the strike price for each stock. It is normal to apply it to stock options, but this is not very specific when considering index options or adjusted stock options. In both cases, it is better to consider the value of the options package as simple:

- Price of exercise × Multiplier

A stock option package usually includes 100 shares. When the rights of the sales contract are exercised, the owner of the stock option receives the exercise price multiplied by the multiplier options - usually 100. The value that the holder of the put option receives is also called the *Option Pack Exercise Price*. Other terms that you may see for this value include:

- Assignment value of the options package
- Optional package delivery value

It depends on which side of the option you are on. All of these terms mean the same thing, the money that is traded when the rights to an appeal or a sales contract are actually exercised.

Protect a portfolio. . . completely

To further discuss the coverage, it is useful to use the alternative range from 0 to +100 and from 0 to -100 for the delta. Indeed, action has a delta of 1. Using this information and ABC's example, Oct. 25, with a delta of -0.186, provides the almost perfect coverage for 19 ABC actions.

ATM calls typically have deltas slightly above 0.50, while ATM investments are typically slightly below 0.50. The use of 0.50 as an approach is generally good for the initial evaluation of the strategy.

Stock hedge

Starting with a perfect stock cover using ABC, let's say you've allocated about $ 5,000 for a combined position (more stock). Since ABC trades at $ 37.50, you expect to own about 100 shares. Using the ABC option data, you focus on the January 35 exercise price option with a five-month maturity. The put gives a delta of -29.1. Since the three put options do not cover 100 stocks, you evaluate a potential position using four put options. The delta for four versions from January 35 is:

- Delta position = number of contracts × Delta = 4 × (-29.1) = -116.4

Like 1 action at +1 delta, a long position of 100 shares represents +100 deltas. A perfectly protected position has a combined delta of zero, requiring 116 ABC actions. You calculate the position delta as follows:

- 116 shares × +1 delta/share = +116 deltas
- 4 whores × -29.1 deltas per put = -116.4 deltas
- Delta position = +116 + (-116.4) = -0.4 Deltas

The cost of the job is calculated as follows:

- 116 shares × $ 37.50 = $ 4350
- 4 positions × $ 1.35 × 100 = $ 540
- Cost of the position = $ 4350 + 540 = $ 4890

This nearly perfect coverage will not stay intact for long; every time the ABC goes up or down by $ 1, the delta changes to approximately its gamma value. Part IV proposes ways to take advantage of this changing situation.

Remember that the delta of an option is changed by range for every $ 1 change in the underlying stock. For this reason, the options are called for *delta* security *variables*. The delta of action, on the other hand, remains constant. A long portion of the shares will also represent one delta is called *the fixed delta* security.

Portfolio hedge

You approach a perfect portfolio hedge the same way, but the fact that not all portfolios are perfectly correlated with an index is problematic. The perfect hedge becomes difficult to reach because the option delta changes as the value of the index changes, and there is an incorrect movement between the index and the portfolio.

Using a delta approach to protect the portfolio of $ 150,000 will bring you closer to a perfect hedge against the strike price estimate. Using an index level of 682, March 690 sales are ITM 8 points. The market price for these sales is $ 20.85, which corresponds to a delta of -0.549. One of the goals is to get closer to 1: 1 protection, so the March 2, 690 purchase gives the following results:

- 2 × 690 × 100 = $ 138,000
- 2 × -0.549 = -1.10

In this case, for every 1 point decrease in OEX, the value of the combined sales increases by 1.1. Over a short period, this translates into 1.1 times the protection of a $ 138,000 portfolio. The multiplication of $ 138,000 by 1.1 provides protection for a portfolio valued at $ 151,800. Given the variable nature of the delta of an option, you will probably be satisfied with slightly less precise portfolio protection.

AVOIDING ADJUSTED OPTION RISK

The adjusted options are those that existed when certain securities transactions took place. As a result of these actions, the terms of the contract required adjustments to reflect the action. Commercial activities that may require it include:

- Share divisions
- Significant cash dividend distributions
- Mergers and Acquisitions
- Spin-off

Most dividends do not result in an option contract adjustment.

Justify option adjustments

The two main reasons why options are adjusted after different securities transactions are:

- To ensure that existing contracts retain their value
- As a result, the contract reflects the securities transaction in your delivery package.

Without modifications, the stock option market could be riskier. Maybe exciting is the right word. . . Imagine one of your calls losing all its value after a stock split and a doubling put option after the distribution of a large cash dividend.

Corporate action 1: Stock splits

Adjustments due to stock split is the fastest to understand. When a stock you own divides two by one (2: 1), you get one additional share for each share you take on the record date - the date used to identify existing shareholders. The day you receive the additional interest, there is nothing very different for the company in terms of its financial statements. To properly evaluate the stock, its price is halved in the market on the day of the stock break.

Option adjustments resulting from a 2: 1 stock split are treated in the same way as stock splits:

- The number of contracts held is modified (similar to shares)
- The price at which the owner has rights (strike price) is adjusted

A new option agreement is created to deal with this corporate transaction and receives a new symbol. When you have an option with the underlying stock going through a 2: 1 split, you will see 2 new option contracts in your account for every 1 contract you had before.

In the current nomenclature of option symbols, the adjusted options are almost indistinguishable from the ordinary options. The problem arises when the delivery option or multiplier has to change to reflect securities trading, which is the case with a 3: 2 split. Modifying an option after a 3: 2 split requires many more adjustments to get the correct score.

When you make a sale without keeping the underlying stock in your account, you create a short position. In fact, the sales rights allow you to sell the underlying shares at the exercise price of the contract. Selling a stock that doesn't belong to you reverses the typical order of a stock transaction and leads to a short position.

Corporate Action 2: Mergers, Splits, and Dividends

Major mergers, acquisitions, spin-offs, and cash dividends change the underlying set of options when an option contract is adjusted. Indeed, the 100 original shares can now represent the delivery of the owner to:

- 100 original shares + shares acquired (merger)
- 100 original shares + new shares (split)
- 100 original shares + cash surrender value (large cash dividend)
- No original shares + acquisition shares (acquired)

In the latter case, the underlying stock may not exist if the company was acquired by another company. Adjusted options are now based on a share of the company that acquired it.

If you think you have found a business option that seems too good to be true, you may very well have stumbled on an option play. Traders on the stock exchanges that are very familiar with corporate actions taken by the actions they negotiate and know how to evaluate adjustments. There is no free money on Wall Street, so do not go into these options without understanding them.

The way you value this type of contract adjustment is more complex. It is essential to understand your rights, obligations, and position assessments if your contract is adjusted. Contact your broker if this happens. And never create, ever a new job using an adjusted option contract that you do not fully understand.

Whenever a combined position (option plus stock) you have is adjusted, be extremely careful when exiting the stock or option position separately. The combined position maintains the appropriate stock option indices created initially, but by selling a portion of the adjusted equity position , you can create great risk in the option position. Talk to your broker to discuss any position changes.

ADJUSTING FROM ADJUSTMENTS

It's good for option markets to have a way to approach contract valuations and delivery packages for different corporate actions, but what does this mean to you? Two things:

When reviewing the adjusted options in your account, check the contract specifications to understand your new rights or obligations, if any.

More importantly, be aware of the adjusted options when creating new positions to evaluate traded securities properly and know their rights and obligations.

Whenever an option quote does not look right, check the details of the contract.

Avoid building new option positions by making use of adjusted options. There is no money hidden in these contracts, just an extra effort to understand and evaluate them.

Detection of an adjusted option

The Options Symbology Initiative proposes a revised approach to option symbols that should more clearly identify the adjusted options. Until all option chains switch to the proposed system, you must know how to detect the adjusted options. Here are some things to check:

- An abbreviation "ADJ" that appears after the symbol in a quote.
- An option root symbol different from the default root
- The optional parcel details may be partially listed with the quote header - see the full quote for any changes to the package
- An exercise price appears twice a month with different symbols.
- Atypical exercise price appears for one share (46375)
- The market price of the options seems to be offline, high or low

These are the main ways to distinguish market-adjusted options. As for all safety, when something does not seem right in terms of price or volume, be sure to dig deeper to see why this is the case.

Evaluating your adjusted options according to the distribution

When an option is modified due to a 2: 1 split, new contracts are valued in the same way as ordinary options. Atypical divisions, like a 3: 2 division, need a little more attention. To evaluate an option after a 3: 2 split:

- Use the adjusted strike price and the multiplier to calculate the value of the set (JKL 60: 60 × 150 = 9000 bonds).
- Determine the underlying package value in the market using current quotes (150 JKL × 62 $ = 9,300 shares).
- Subtract the value of the package from the market value to obtain the intrinsic value of the option ($ 9,300 - 9,000 = $ 300).
- Assuming an option quote of $ 3, what remains after subtracting the intrinsic value is the the extrinsic value ($ 3 × 150 = $ 450, $ 450 - 300 = $ 150).

While people often think of markets moving in one of two possible directions, they also spend a lot of time moving in a third direction: laterally. Individual averages, sectors, and headings show different degrees of trend (up or down) and trend (side).

Option strategies are unique in that they allow you to make a profit when lateral movement is in place. By using options, you can earn additional rewards on existing positions or trade-in limited-risk markets. Long butterflies and condors are two of the strategies presented here.

WINNING POSITIONS IN SIDEWAYS MARKETS

You have two dilemmas when markets move laterally:

- Manage stagnant returns from existing positions
- How to win new positions

You may be agitated when lateral movement persists, asking if you should close your current positions and when things will go back (and in which direction). Although I do not know the exact statistics on the time the market goes into the "no-trend" mode, I know that because I negotiate options, it does not really matter. First, consider the management of positions when the market stabilizes in a parallel trading range.

MANAGE EXISTING POSITIONS

Long calls allow you to earn gains with rising trends, while long options allow you to earn gains with declining trends. When markets spend time moving sideways, you can make gains by matching positions. I hope you are now contented with the combined positions, as there are so many different ones available. As a starting point, options can be included in existing stocks or exchange-traded funds (ETFs) to increase returns when markets seem insane.

As a general rule, to start new positions, you want to sell a premium when the implied volatility is relatively high and purchase it when it is relatively low.

COMMENTS ON THE STRATEGY

It turns out that DELL had a daily shutdown further below the lower regression channel line at the end of July 2002 and that some fences over the upper regression channel at the beginning of November 2002, before eventually May 2003. The price remained in the range of channels except for a few days for 18 months.

The covered call strategy could have continued to generate profits throughout this period. If the shares were withdrawn during the May 2003 break, they could have been redeemed later in the month, when DELL returned to test the upper line of the channel, which now serves as support.

Do not place a permanent stop-loss order for the underlying stocks used in a hedged purchase strategy. If the stop is triggered, you will have a short call naked, which is an unlimited risk position.

In reviewing the DELL case study, I hope you have noted the following important points:

The short call does not protect the position of the stock; generally, only reduces the cost base, which moderately reduces the risk

You must minimize your risk by identifying a stop loss output level, even if it means buying a short purchase out of stock

Historical volatility and implied volatility generally decrease when security is within a trading range.

Earnings reports and other news related to the economy and society can significantly affect the implied volatility, even when the price moves essentially laterally.

You should consider your vision long term of the position on the shares long term because there is a limited potential loss but higher with this strategy.

As an alternative approach, it is possible to buy a long-term put while calls are sold each month to protect the disadvantages.

Cash Closing Calls (ITCs) can be launched for one month and increase the exercise price to a modest gain when stocks increase

Commissions can have a significant impact on business results

Other business costs, such as tax consequences, must be taken into account when implementing this strategy or any business strategy.

Trading rules based on stop loss exits and regression channel breaks help implement a successful strategy in risk management.

portfolio trading provides problems that can occur when in working a new strategy, as the impact of the IV compared to the price of time

When a long-term consolidation leak occurs, it is common for the stock to come back to test the model.

If you leave or are called from a position when implementing a covered call strategy during a consolidation, a return to the default value may provide the opportunity to establish a new directional position in the 'inventory.

A LEAPS contract is a long-term option obtainable for certain underlying indices, exchange-traded funds, and equities. These contracts generally have more than nine months to 21/2 years to expire and become regular options once this period has elapsed.

By selling calls on long stocks or the ETF position, you increase the number of ways in which stocks can move while allowing gains. You also reduce your potential gains if an upside-down explosive movement occurs. It's just a strategy exchange that you need to consider when considering different business approaches.

Option Strategies for Lateral Movements

The covered purchase strategy is only one that can generate gains during the parallel trading periods. As mentioned in the comments on the strategy, you can choose to protect the stock position with a long put option, and then sell the calls monthly until a break occurs or the expiration month of the long sale is over. approach.

In addition to the combination of stock positions and options, you can extend the same concept to a single combination of options using LEAPS contract positions (long term stock anticipation shares) on the leg of the venue. Action. This approach generally reduces the risk by reducing the total cost of the position.

Risk management occurs before generating revenue. If you experience a prolonged lateral movement of a title you hold, you can create a lower perspective for action, move out of position, or protect with a put.

What to consider with the combinations of options

One of the benefit options generally on individual stocks and exchange-traded funds (ETFs) that underlie the options is that they generally require less investment. The bottom line is that you have less money at risk. The disadvantage is that any asset can expire worthlessly. And this is for you on the commercial side - there are a number of things to consider for each type of asset you decide to use. That's why managing your risk is a common thread. The only collateral considered risk free is a US Treasury Note.

When a stock moves laterally for a period, it is said to be in the consolidation phase. The greater the consolidation, the greater the chances of a strong leadership moving away from this consolidation.

Instead of a portfolio of individual stocks or ETFs, you can keep LEAPS contracts for different stocks or sectors. A covered call strategy may be applied using the LEAPS option as a secondary mobile asset from which you increase your revenue. There are little things to consider if you follow this path:

Using a LEAPS contract as the underlying will subject you to margin requirements since the position technically represents a spread, not a pure short position covered.

Spread strategies require a different level of option approval from your broker - you may be able to access these strategies or not, depending on your type of account (for example, IRAs).

Since LEAPS are also subject to the same price factors as an ordinary option contract, Implied Volatility (IV) conditions favorable to the sale of calls are not necessarily ideal for LEAPS purchases. The strategy can work better on an existing job.

The double-edged sword IV may result in conditions in which it is better to sell your LEAPS contract, which may have decreased less than the underlying asset itself.

In addition to a LEAPS strategy, additional revenue can be generated from a calendar strategy simply by using an existing long call. In this case, the short-term calls are sold against a long call by the underlying. The risk is moderately reduced by reducing your net position investment, and the same considerations apply to those listed for a short call LEAPS approach.

The term deployment option refers to the process in which an existing option position is closed by a clearing transaction, and a similar new position is created for a month later.

Strategy short-list

Some of the strategies discussed in this book that can provide gains in secondary markets, moderately reduce risk, or both, include:

- Purchase of long-term shares (limited but high-risk position)
- Credit spread (a little money)
- Put the credit gap (a little money)
- Calendar of calls
- Put the calendar
- Distribution of the call ratio (unlimited risk position)
- Increase the sale rate (limited-risk position, but high risk)

Here are two limited risk strategies designed specifically to benefit from secondary market action - the butterfly and the condor.

Understanding Butterfly Positions

A butterfly is a strategy designed specifically to win when security or ETF trades sideways. Some features of the strategy are:

- Limited risk and limited reward
- Can be created using calls or put
- Combines two vertical gaps
- It's short term in nature
- Usually created for a debt

Maximize gains when the underlying security remains within a trading range dictated by option strike prices

A variation of the basic butterfly is the iron butterfly that combines calls and bets. This post is usually created for a time-saving credit in your favor .

A market in lateral movement can also be called without trend or direction.

DEFINING THE LONG BUTTERFLY

As with some of the strategies discussed in this book, the butterfly comes in two varieties:

- Butterfly long call
- Long butterfly

Both strategies combine a vertical credit spread, and a vertical debit spread to capitalize on lateral market movements. The policy name comes from the three options used to create the item, as follows:

- Body: 2 short options of similar type
- Wing 1: a much lower exercise price option
- Wing 2: a much higher exercise price option

Generally , the price of exercise of the options are short in cash (ATM) or near-cash, profits are maximized if the underlying closes below to maturity in the exercise price of the short options.

Always consider different strategies adapted to current market conditions. You may decide that an alternative strategy better reduces your risk.

Creation of an iron butterfly

The long iron butterfly is a touch of service and places butterflies that allow you to create a position for a credit. To do this, you use a redemption spread and a rising spread, both for credit. The position remains with limited risk and limited reward. He also has lateral movements to maximize the gains. In the "you get nothing for nothing" category, these spreads require an extra margin because the two vertical spreads are credit positions.

The put and call butterfly

The Iron Butterfly combines two vertical credit spreads to capitalize on the lateral movement of stock as follows:

- A bearish buying spread with an exercise price of the close short or cash option (ATM)
- An upward selling spread with an exercise price close to short or ATM and the same exercise price of short purchase

Brokers can base their margin requirements on the iron butterfly on a short overlap-strangling combination instead of two vertical credit spreads. Check with your broker for specific requirements before creating a position.

Vertical spread spreads are the same for both credit spreads; The maximum risk for the position is the difference in the exercise price of a vertical spread less than the initial credit. The long iron butterfly has exercise prices that line up like this:

- The lowest strike price is a long option.
- The next lowest exercise price is a short sale.
- The same exercise price is used for a short call.
- The highest strike price is a long decision.

When creating the iron butterfly, you use the same exercise price for the short option. The initial credit you get to establish the position is your maximum reward.

Risk of the iron butterfly

Making use of an iron butterfly with a wider spread minimizes the risk-reward rate for this position. The following example uses an action that typically moves more silently (historical volatility at 100 days - 12%), with slightly lower levels of implied volatility (IV) over the past 12 months.

Securities transactions may lead to adjustments to existing option contracts. Be sure to check the specifications of the options you use, especially when prices seem low.

Example of a long iron butterfly

We are in mid-June, and after a sharp drop in equities three months ago, the MO has returned to a more distinctive trading range. It turned out that there was a fallout

This changed the valuation of the company. The MO is trading around $ 70 and, having decided that the split should not have an impact on stocks in the future, you evaluate the following iron butterfly:

- Long 1 Jul.60 Put @ $ 0.05

- Short July 1 70 Put @ $ 1.20
- Enjoy July 1, 70 Call at $ 1.30
- July 1, 80 Long calls @ $ 0.05

Therefore, instead of a $ 3 spread on the index shares trading around $ 106, you have improved the spread to $ 10 on a $ 70 share.

An iron butterfly combines four different options - be sure to consider your trading fees before entering a position.

By calculating the net credit for these options, you get the following credit, which is your maximum reward:

- Bear Call Spread Credit + Bull Selling Spread Credit

Since both spreads have the same distance, the maximum risk is the difference between the two strike prices minus the initial credit.

[(Exercise price difference × 100)] - Initial credit

[(80 - 70) - $ 240] = $ 760

Butterflies and condors have two levels of balance - one up and one down.

The once esoteric world of options is now present in the investment community. Yes, we may have heard cynical and negative statements about this mysterious derivative, "oh, so risky!" But, like any type of investment product, the risk is purely relative. And having a solid foundation and understanding of this product, often viewed negatively, is the key to mastering and maximizing this tool in the investment portfolio. The versatility of the options, which allows traders to take advantage of the three types of markets (high, low, and stagnant), has made option trading an extremely attractive tool for many. Formerly only available to institutional traders and investors, options trading has become widespread in the market, and the arrival of online brokers has made trading of these complex derivatives accessible to retail investors.

The investors in the stock options generally buy stock options in lieu of long and short positions. Even though these options are priced at a small fraction of the actual inventory, statistics have shown that most of these options are really worthless. In essence, this means a loss of 100% of the prepaid premium.

Does this make option trading extremely dangerous? It depends. In fact, you can use this leveraged product to generate passive income! Sounds good? Let me share some of the techniques that cautious investors use to generate passive income from trading options.

PUT OPTIONS

To hedge against the significant capital losses in their portfolios, especially in a downward trend, some investors would adopt a strategy of "protective sale" as a form of management technique of risk. This strategy essentially consists in maintaining a put option in addition to the investor's existing equity position, which decreases his risk of losing money if the value of the stock is unfavorable to him.

However, a put option expires with time. Therefore, to minimize its losses on its portfolio, the investor should continually buy put options to ensure his portfolio is secure.

For example, one person currently owns 1,000 ABC shares for $ 10 each. To protect his shares from unlimited risk, he may want to buy 10 sales contracts (because 1 option contract gives the buyer the right, not the obligation to sell 100 shares) at the exercise price of $ 9. for a premium. starting at $ 1.50 * 100 * 10 = $ 1500 (for ten option contracts). In the event that the value of ABC falls to $ 5, the investor is entitled to exercise his option contracts to sell his shares for $ 9 each.

GENERATE MONTHLY PROFITS WITH PUT OPTIONS

Although put options are primarily used by institutions and investors as a form of hedging tool, they can also serve as a means to generate passive income! By selling put options that expire in a month, you can regularly earn a premium (paid by the option buyer)!

Suppose an investor has an increase in ABC stock, which currently costs $ 50. To take advantage of rising or stagnant stock, he may actually sell a put option on a strike that is less than the actual value of the stock (for example). for example, $ 45) and win a prize for it. Be careful, however, by selling a put, the person is really "naked" in his position and exposed to unlimited losses.

For a conservative investor, he can decide to buy a new put option to attack even lower (e . G. $ 40) and pay a premium that is lower than the price he got from the sale of the previous option in the $ 45 exercise, which allows him to earn the difference between the two prices from the outset. In this scenario, the maximum investor losses are limited to $ 5 if the stock price falls below $ 40.

CALL OPTIONS

As with the put option, some investors who sell less than the market may buy put options to avoid exposure to a positive risk. However, most investors buy call options for speculative purposes. Potential positive returns augmented by the leverage offered by option trading make this tool extremely attractive to low-income investors who may want to make quick money and take advantage of a potential uptrend.

GENERATING MONTHLY PROFITS WITH CALL OPTIONS

Similar to the previous strategy of selling put options, the idea here is to sell call options that expire in a month.

Here is an example:

Suppose an investor has a delisting on the ABC stock, which currently costs $ 100. To take advantage of low or stagnant share, it can actually sell a call option in the event of the strike, then the value of the action (e.g., $ 105) and win a prize for it. Again, by trading a call   option, the investor is exposed to unlimited losses.

A prudent investor can choose to buy a new option called for an attack more (e . G. $ 110) and pay a premium that is lower than the price he got from the sale of the previous option in the exercise of $

105. This allows him to win the difference between the two prizes from the start. In this scenario, your maximum losses are limited to $ 5, even if the stock price exceeds $ 110.

COVERED-CALL STRATEGY

Unlike the previous strategy of selling calls without actually owning the actual stock, a hedged call strategy is adopted when an investor owns shares of the purchase he sells. This strategy is often utilized when an investor has a short-term, neutral view of the stock. As a result, the investor would continue to buy the stock while reducing the call option to generate additional earnings from the option premium.

Again, take the example of Apple Inc., which is currently valued at $ 705.02. Suppose an investor currently owns 200 Apple stocks and has a neutral view of the company in the short term (months). He can choose to sell 2 strike calls of $ 710 or $ 715 (if he is more risk-averse) to earn 2 * 15.2 * 100 = $ 3040 and 2 * 12.95 * 100 = 2 $ 590, respectively. The following shows the potential result on the due date:

AAPL shares remain stable – option will expire worthlessly, and the power of investors will keep the premium acquired from the sale of the option.

AAPL Increase - If the stock price exceeds the strike, the option is exercised, and the investor's capital gains on his shares are limited to $ 710 or $ 715 (depending on the strike chosen).

AAPL shares fall - the option will expire worthlessly, and the investor will be able to retain the premium earned on the sale of the option.

This means that 2 of 3 scenarios would make the investor a winner! The only opposite side of this strategy would be to lose the upside potential due to the sale of the call option. Whatever it is, the majority of investors choose to sell your option at a strike, which they felt to ease the sale of their real actions. This makes this strategy a win-win situation!

Conclusion

The sale of put options or a call can be a great addition to a well-diversified portfolio as it let investors generate passive income regularly. Keep in mind, however, that put options expose you to unlimited risk if they are not protected.

For conservative or new investors, it is important first to recognize the maximum amount of risk you are willing to take on a trade and develop a strategy for selling and buying put / sell options (also known as the spread) to mitigate their losses.

There are no secrets in this world, there is only a lot of work and a lot of study. Reread this book at least 5 times because the information is a lot, and powerful.

If you don't, you won't understand the importance of this book.

All this works, during covid-19 I made money thanks to this method, so don't stop, read the book again and start earning!

I invite you to leave a positive review on amazon. If you do, I will notify you for future updates regarding this book and new information.

Thank you.

Made in the USA
Monee, IL
14 August 2020